To my good friend, Eupha

With Love,

Mamie J.

Christmas 1975

FRIEND GIFT

FRIEND GIFT

Perry Tanksley

FLEMING H. REVELL COMPANY

OLD TAPPAN, NEW JERSEY

Scripture quotations in this volume are from *The Living Bible*—Tyndale House Publishers, Illinois. Used by permission.

The poems in this volume were written by Perry Tanksley.

Library of Congress Cataloging in Publication Data

Tanksley, Perry.
  Friend gift.

  Poems.
  I. Title.
PS3570.A53F7   811'.5'4   72-4412
ISBN 0-8007-0552-1

Contents

FRIEND GIFT

...for the pleasures we've shared.

When hearts are reaching out
And affection is real
And fingertips are touching
Then tell it if you will.
For there's no better time
To say so none can doubt
Exactly how you feel
When hearts are reaching out.
But if you fail that moment
And let your heart grow cold,
You sin against yourself
And the one you never told.
Then express your feelings now
Lest you go cruelly crushing
The tender blossoms of love
That bloom when lives are touching.

How to Win and Keep a Friend

Work happily together. Don't try to act big. Don't try
to get into the good graces of important people, but
enjoy the company of ordinary folks. And don't think
you know it all!   Romans 12:16

OUR LIVES ARE TOUCHING

Of things that mean the most
And of things that mean much,
The most meaningful thing is
When lives of friends touch.
For something very special
Which I cannot define
Occurred in my living
When your heart touched mine.
Memories of that moment
Now cling without my clutching,
And every day grows sweeter
Because our lives are touching.

A DO-IT-YOURSELF FAITH

I begged my God to give
To me a sincere friend,
But He gave love and said,
"Each one his own must win."
I dreamed a dream and prayed
That war and strife would cease,
But God said, "I've given you
A voice to speak for peace."
When I prayed, "Smooth my path,
Replace my dingy hovel;"
God only gave me tools—
A hammer, saw, and shovel.

HE ONLY HAD SOME GOLD

I saw him everyday
And he possessed a flair
To swing a business deal
And be a millionaire.
He was with zeal obsessed
To muster this world's wealth,
Though it caused him at last
To lose his friends and health.
At last success was his
While I, deprived, sought most
To be enriched with friends,
And now I, too, can boast.
Life gave us all we asked
But how can one explain,
Why my friend of wealth
Of lonely days complains.
Life paid us what we sought
For both of us grew old.
I only had some friends.
He only had some gold.

*If you love your neighbor as much as you love
yourself you will not want to harm or cheat
him, or kill him or steal from him. And you
won't sin with his wife or want what is his, or
do anything else the Ten Commandments say
is wrong. All ten are wrapped up in this one,
to love your neighbor as you love yourself.*
                                    Romans 13:9

How to Make Faith Effective

Don't hide your light! Let it shine for all; let your good
deeds glow for all to see, so that they will praise your
heavenly Father.   Matthew 5:15, 16

SIX SERMONS WALKING

I didn't go to church this week—
I missed the preacher's talking,
But I have had my deep needs met
I've seen six sermons walking.
I glimpsed some children caroling
With faces sweet and kind,
But when I stopped to hear them singing,
I noticed they were blind.
Where icy streets crossed, I beheld
A white youth turn his back
On friends to help a woman cross
And she was stooped and black.
Outside a home for unwed mothers
I saw an unwanted child
Placed in a childless couple's care;
You should have seen them smile.
I passed a crippled paper boy
Hobbling on crutches and braces,
And he was shouting, "Merry Christmas,"
To all the business places.
I saw a man, retired and poor,
Giving his coat away
To a drunk man half-frozen
On a shivering winter's day.
Along a dingy street I saw
A Christian worker embrace
A runaway, spaced out on drugs,
And tears poured down each face.
I didn't get to church this week—
I seldom miss it, indeed,
But I beheld six sermons walking
And they have met my need.

THE TRAGEDY

To have existed uncaring
For X number of nights and morns
Is a more dreadful fate
Than to have never been born.
To have looked indifferently
At stars shining through pines
Is a tragedy more cruel
Than to have been born blind.
To have listened unhearing
The symphony of songbirds
Is an affliction worse than
To have never really heard.
To have existed unloving
For X number of springs and falls
Is a misfortune sadder than
To have never lived at all.

You are the world's seasoning, to make it tolerable. If you lose your flavor, what will happen to the world? And you yourselves will be thrown out and trampled underfoot as worthless.   Matthew 5:13

Dear foolish man! When will you ever learn that "believing" is useless without doing what God wants you to? Faith that does not result in good deeds is not real faith.   James 2:20

For every child of God can obey Him, defeating sin and evil pleasure by trusting Christ to help him. But who could possibly fight and win this battle except by believing that Jesus is truly the Son of God?

1 John 4, 5

VICTORY IS PROMISED

Because I've tasted life—
Its blessing and its cursing,
I now know nothing ever
Defeats a Christian person.
Not that we aren't distressed.
The world of sin overwhelms,
But though cast down we're sure
Of victory in these realms.
Not that we triumph daily—
Some days we're virtually beat,
But Christian people never
Experience total defeat.
And triumph means much more
Than mere daily surviving
Or acquiescing to
The hopelessness of striving.
Such is a hollow victory
Existence—but not living;
In Christ we have new life
Forgiven and forgiving.
I am possessed today
By one compelling conviction:
In Christ I'm more than conqueror.
Nothing defeats a Christian.

So take a new grip with your tired hands, stand firm on your shaky legs, And mark out a straight, smooth path for your feet so that those who follow you, though weak and lame, will not fall and hurt themselves, but become strong. Hebrews 12:12, 13

I DARE YOU TO TRY IT

What if every day
You recounted your fears,
And recited your aches,
And recalled your tears?
Life would be drudgery—
An unbearable duty,
And remembering grudges
There would be no beauty.
What if every day
We thought good things,
And counted our blessings
Instead of our stings.
I dare you to try it
And cling to the beautiful,
But not if you object to
Growing daily more youthful.

So don't worry at all about having enough food and clothing. Why be like the heathen? For they take pride in all these things and are deeply concerned about them. But your heavenly Father already knows perfectly well that you need them, And He will gladly give them to you if you give Him first place in your life. So don't be anxious about tomorrow. God will take care of your tomorrow too. Live one day at a time. Matthew 6:31–34

But when you ask Him, be sure that you really expect Him to tell you, for a doubtful mind will be as unsettled as a wave of the sea that is driven and tossed by the wind . . . . James 1:6

THE FOOTPRINTS OF GOD

On a mountain camping trip,
One morn outside our camp,
I saw fresh-made bear tracks
Impressed in clay half-damp.
Of course, the bears had fled
But I with fresh footprints
Could prove bears had been there
None could be unconvinced.
In fields and woods and streams
I've seen God's footprints clear,
And though I've not seen God
Yet I know He's been here.
That's why my faith in God
Springs up like crystal fountains
When I see footprints imprinted
On valleys, seas, and mountains.

NO SIN TO QUESTION

If it were wrong to ask the question *why*
Then Jesus sinned when He went forth to die,
For on a cross set bold against the sky
He in His weakest moment asked *why*.
Could it be wrong to die inquiring
Why You are falsely accused,
Or to hate the cross and spikes employed
Or even the sword they used.
It is not wrong to question suffering.
I think it's proof of faith.
Nor does it mean one questions God
It's proof of saving grace.
No moment in the Master's ministry
Shines with more brilliant flash
Than when the Son of Man asked *why*
And begged the cup to pass.

Then He asked them, "Where is your faith?"
And they were filled with awe and fear of Him
and said to one another, "Who is this man,
that even the winds and waves obey Him?"
Luke 8:25

You may as well know this too, Timothy, that
in the last days it is going to be very difficult
to be a Christian. 2 Timothy 3:1

How to Face the Future With Hope

For I live in eager expectation and hope that I will never do anything that will cause me to be ashamed of myself but that I will always be ready to speak out boldly for Christ while I am going through all these trials here, just as I have in the past; and that I will always be an honor to Christ, whether I live or whether I must die.

Philippians 1:20

I'LL START TOMORROW FRESH

Not just once a year—
Each day a fresh beginning
Is at my fingertips
For me to start winning.
Why should I wait all year
Until December ends?
Tonight I'll close the ledger.
Tomorrow I'll start again.
I'll start tomorrow fresh,
And cleansed by new resolves
I'll celebrate New Year
As each new dawn evolves.

No, dear brothers, I am still not all I should be but I am bringing all my energies to bear on this one thing: Forgetting the past and looking forward to what lies ahead. I strain to reach the end of the race and receive the prize for which God is calling us up to heaven because of what Christ Jesus did for us.

Philippians 3:13, 14

The courage of many people will falter because of the fearful fate they see coming upon the earth, for the stability of the very heavens will be broken up. Then the peoples of the earth shall see Me, the Man from Heaven, coming in a cloud with power and great glory. So when all these things begin to happen, stand straight and look up! For your salvation is near. Luke 21:26–28

HOLD TO THE HAPPINESS YOU HAVE

If with the tip of your fingers
You've brushed happiness lightly,
Or even grasped it partially
Or gripped it tightly,
Then do not do as fools do
And let it casually slip
Beyond your hands and plummet
From unheeding fingertips.
Hold to the happiness you have
And cling to it and cherish,
For happiness taken for granted
Will slowly but surely perish.

LET US SO LIVE

Where there is work let us labor
Where there is malice—forgive;
Where there is hunger let us share
Where there is dread—let us live.
Where there is grief let us comfort
Where there is anguish—console;
Where there is sadness let us cheer—
Especially the lonely and old.
Where there are lost souls—let us witness.
Where hearts are breaking—heal;
Let us so live, the world, through us
May know that Christ is real.

How to Show Your Love

Don't just pretend that you love others: really love them. Hate what is wrong. Stand on the side of the good. Love each other with brotherly affection and take delight in honoring each other. Never be lazy in your work but serve the Lord enthusiastically.

Romans 12:9–11

IT'S THE MOTIVE THAT COUNTS

It's not the deed
But the thought behind it,
It's not the letter
But the love that signed it.
It's not the flower
But the motive that sent it.
It's not the flattery
But whether you meant it.
It's not the melody
But the words of the hymn
And what you were thinking
When at church you sang them.
God looks at the heart,
And people do, likewise;
It's the motive that counts
And love unseen to eyes.

Be gentle and ready to forgive; never hold grudges. Remember, the Lord forgave you, so you must forgive others. Most of all, let love guide your life for then the whole church will stay together in perfect harmony.

Colossians 3:13, 14

Dear brothers, if a Christian is overcome by some sin, you who are godly should gently and humbly help him back onto the right path, remembering that next time it might be one of you who is in the wrong. Galatians 6:1

THE LIGHT

He groped along our street
Tapping softly with his cane,
And as he went he held
A light none could explain.
"But why the light?" I asked.
I knew he could not see.
He smiled, "It's so my friends
Won't stumble over me."
Touched deeply by this, I prayed,
"Lord, though my light is small,
Help me to let it shine,
Lest I cause friends to fall."

FRIENDSHIP

Somehow you understood my moods
And sensed my deeper needs;
You tried to smooth my rocky path
Performing golden deeds.
But it was loyalty you proved
In my most recent loss
That made me thankful God allowed
Your path and mine to cross.

How to Deal With Disappointment

These troubles and sufferings of ours are, after all, quite small and won't last very long. Yet this short time of distress will result in God's richest blessing upon us forever and ever! 2 Corinthians 4:17

FAITH TO STICK

I've tried so hard, Lord,
And I'm not denying
That oftentimes I've cried
Disappointed from trying.
But thoughts of quitting, Lord,
As I so often planned it
Now make me feel such shame
That I can hardly stand it.
Lord, grant me faith to stick
And not to flee temptation
As you in Gethsemane
Deserted not your station.

AN UNVENTURING FAILURE

Between the boy I used to be
And the man I might have been
Is the disappointment I am—
Unkind and vain within.
Sometimes I ask, "Why have I failed
To be the noble man
Of which I dreamed long years ago?
What happened to my plan?"
Doubtless I've failed to measure up
To my ambitious thoughts,
And fallen short of youthful dreams
And missed high goals I sought.
Between the boy I used to be
And my vision so gallant
Is an unventuring failure,
Cowardly hiding his talent.

WHERE I FOUND HELP

Although my loss is great
I keep on keeping on,
For I gain strength from God,
Treading the meadows alone.
In grief and tears can one
Be sure he has the goods?
Yet God's love consoles me
When I weave through the woods.
Sorrow has crushed completely
Yet I, despite my loss,
Have found the comfort needed
While kneeling at the cross.

Always be thankful no matter what happens, for that is God's will for you who belong to Christ Jesus. 1 Thessalonians 5:18

And we know that all that happens to us is working for our good if we love God and are fitting into His plans. Romans 8:28

But if any of you causes one of these little ones who trusts in Me to lose his faith, it would be better for you to have a rock tied to your neck and be thrown into the sea. Woe upon the world for all its evils. Temptation to do wrong is inevitable, but woe to the man who does the tempting.   Matthew 18:6, 7

BOTH SIDES OF MY MOUTH

Lord, it's not that I don't know
The right from wrong these days;
It's just that I lack the courage
To choose the right always.
And it's not that I don't know
What I should stand up for;
It's just that I waver back and forth—
Debating *either or.*
And I know truth from error,
But spiritual blight and drought
Have made me expert at talking
Out of both sides of my mouth.

I'D RATHER BE A HEATHEN

I'd rather have a pagan's creed
And think with pagan mind
Than know by heart the law of Christ
And live a life unkind.
I'd rather be a heathen man
With manners all uncouth,
Than memorize the creed of Christ
And then betray His truth.
I'd rather live without a faith
And die in ignorance dumb,
Than know of Christ and then live life
As if He hadn't come.

HYPOCRISY

As Christ once climbed the Mount
Of His transfiguration,
So now He climbs again
To share new revelations.
And as He knelt and prayed
With Peter, John, and James,
So fresh Gethsemanes
Still beckon us the same.
Yet we refuse to kneel,
Though we still mouth His creed,
And few ascend the Mount;
We hardly sense our need.

But the Holy Spirit tells us clearly that in the last times some in the church will turn away from Christ and become eager followers of teachers with devil-inspired ideas. These teachers will tell lies with straight faces and do it so often that their consciences won't even bother them.   1 Timothy 4:1, 2

Remember that some men, even pastors, lead sinful lives and everyone knows it. In such situations you can do something about it. But in other cases only the judgment day will reveal the terrible truth.   1 Timothy 5:24

How to Help Others

Share each other's troubles and problems, and so obey our Lord's command. If anyone thinks he is too great to stoop to this, he is fooling himself. He is really a nobody.   Galatians 6:2, 3

BECAUSE YOU TALKED TO ME

When I was so in need
Somehow you chanced to call
And you just talked to me
And I felt ten feet tall.
You didn't know my need
Nor could you ever see
The miracle wrought that day
When you just talked to me.
But, friend, I felt courageous
When you left me that day
Because you talked to me
And knew just what to say.

THOUGHTS OF YOU

When I think of you
I think of one to count on,
And someone to lean on,
And a friend true-blue.
When I think of you
I think of helping hands
And someone who understands
With kindness, too.
When I think of you
My prayers rise above
To the Source of all love,
With thanks overdue.
When I think of you
I hope you'll think of me
As one who longs to be
A friend of yours as true.

YOU'RE IN MY HEART

The favor you bestowed
On me in my deep need
Is now to you no doubt
A long forgotten deed.
But I remember it
With gentle words you spoke,
For through these years they've soothed
A heart that sorrow broke.
I can't repay your love
But in my heart you'll find
A hall of fame in which
Your name in gold is signed.

Most important of all, continue to show deep love for each other, for love makes up for many of your faults.   1 Peter 4:8

And why worry about a speck in the eye of a brother when you have a board in your own? Should you say, "Friend, let me help you get that speck out of your eye," when you can't even see because of the board in your own? Hypocrite! First get rid of the board. Then you can see to help your brother.
                                                        Matthew 7:3–5

Peace

A work of art entitled *Peace*
Featured a waterfall,
And by the gorge there grew an oak
And it was aged and tall.
In the crotch of the limb there was
A robin's nest that swayed,
And in the nest over the falls
A robin sang unafraid.
I wondered why the artist
Depicted peace as thus—
A robin's nest—a waterfall.
Is that what God gives us?
To me the answer was obvious
For I'd known threatening dismay,
And felt serene amidst the storm
As trusting birds display.
Beneath us are Arms everlasting,
And facing things dismaying,
I've known the peace the artist meant
And trust like robins swaying.

It is God Himself who has made us what we are and given us new lives from Christ Jesus; and long ages ago He planned that we should spend these lives in helping others. Ephesians 2:10

REJECTED AT HOME

Admiring pulpiteers,
I volunteered to preach,
But Jesus said to me,
"Go witness on your street."
Dejectedly I went
To work so commonplace,
Yet while I witnessed there,
Neighbors laughed in my face.
It was then I felt keenly,
Right in my own hometown,
How Jesus must have felt
When Nazareth turned Him down.

TO WITNESS WITH LIFE

You never mentioned faith
And yet I say sincerely,
I have a stronger faith.
Your life has witnessed clearly.
You never mentioned kindness
And yet in some strange fashion
You've witnessed with your life
Of Christ and His compassion.
You never mentioned Jesus
And how He healed men's blindness,
Yet my blind eyes now see.
Christ healed me through your kindness.

THE SILENT FOLK

The deeper streams in silence flow,
While shallow brooks still babble;
Full ships sink low and empty cars
On railroad tracks still rattle.
The silent folk like silent stars
On darkest nights shine best,
And burdened hearts like ships bowed down
Are still the ones that bless.

Dear brothers, what's the use of saying that you have faith and are Christians if you aren't proving it by helping others? Will that kind of faith save anyone? James 2:14

Take care to live in Me, and let Me live in you. For a branch can't produce fruit when severed from the vine. Nor can you be fruitful apart from Me. Yes, I am the Vine; you are the branches. Whoever lives in Me and I in him shall produce a large crop of fruit. For apart from Me you can't do a thing. John 15:4, 5

How to Think About Christmas

The Christian who is pure and without fault, from God the Father's point of view, is the one who takes care of orphans and widows, and whose soul remains true to the Lord—not soiled and dirtied by its contacts with the world.   James 1:27

NEGLECTED CHILDREN

This year at Christmastide,
Men without full employment
Whose children go neglected,
Prevent my full enjoyment.
This year at Christmastide
I find my meat and bread
Sticking in my throat
Because of those unfed.
And I can hardly eat
The turkey that I carve,
Because of those today
Unloved and cold and starved.
The cry of hungry children
At home and far away
Cancels half my joy
On this December day.

In this new life one's nationality or race or education or social position is unimportant; such things mean nothing. Whether a person has Christ is what matters, and He is equally available to all.   Colossians 3:11

You know how full of love and kindness our Lord Jesus was: though He was so very rich, yet to help you He became so very poor, so that by being poor He could make you rich.
                                  2 Corinthians 8:9

CHRISTMAS FINDS ME SAD

It's Christmas everywhere,
And yet I know a place
Where families sit forlorn
With sadness in their face.
For them no star shines bright,
To them no wise men bring
Gifts for the little children.
For them no angels sing.
I know I should be glad
It's Christmas everywhere,
But Christmas finds me sad
Until it's Christmas there.

THE CHRISTMAS TOUCH

Why not a different kind of Christmas?
Like sharing Christ's love each day,
Like giving ourselves away,
Like calling someone to say,
"I love you very much."
Be done with the ordinary Christmas!
Where joys of Christmas season
Are synonymous with self-pleasing,
And people ignore souls freezing.
Shut out from love, as such.
Why not a Christ-filled Christmas?
Where we are not the center,
But invite the Christ to enter,
That January through December,
We'll feel the Christmas touch.

How to Think of the Saviour

We all know He did not come as an angel but as a human being—yes, a Jew. And it was necessary for Jesus to be like us, His brothers, so that He could be our merciful and faithful High Priest before God, a Priest who would be both merciful to us and faithful to God in dealing with the sins of the people.

Hebrews 2:16, 17

IF I SHOULD FEEL
CONTEMPT

The only way I can display
I love the Lord above
Is by loving the lost world
Which He so dearly loves.
And I must never testify
I'm with Christ in accord
If I dislike the needy
Who really need the Lord.
If I should feel contempt
For those for whom He died,
Then let me claim no more
To love the crucified.

Don't ever forget the wonderful fact that Jesus Christ was a Man, born into King David's family; and that He was God, as shown by the fact that He rose again from the dead.

2 Timothy 2:8

Keep your eyes on Jesus, our leader and instructor. He was willing to die a shameful death on the cross because of the joy He knew would be His afterwards; and now He sits in the place of honor by the throne of God.

Hebrews 12:2

I DREAMED HE CAME

When Jesus came to my house
It took me with surprise,
But I threw open the door
And asked the Lord inside.
At first I thought I'd be
Overwhelmed in His presence—
Unworthy and guilty-like.
Instead I found it pleasant.
I really expected to have
Feelings of remorse and shame
For selfish sinful living,
Instead He called my name.
The only shame I felt
Was that I'd been so fearful
That He would sternly judge.
Instead I found Him cheerful.
Unlike most Christian people,
He loved and called me friend
I knew He liked me, too,
With all my faults and sins.
He's grown so dear to me
His love I'll never doubt,
Since in a dream I welcomed
The Master to my house.

How to Think of God

His purpose in all of this is that they should seek after God, and perhaps feel their way toward Him and find Him—though He is not far from any one of us.

Acts 17:27

THE SORROWING GOD

She pointed to her door and sighed,
"Do you see my gold star?
Where was your God when my boy died
And marched across the bar?
And where was God when my heart cried
And love hung up that star?"
"God's sky is full of stars," said I,
"And they're for soldiers dying,
And He still stands where He once stood
When men were crucifying,
And He still stands with low-bowed head
And He is meekly crying."

A CHRISTLIKE GOD

Who knows what God is like?
My concept is quite dim;
And yet in Christ I think
I've caught a glimpse of Him.
Who comprehends God's love?
Perhaps the very smart;
And yet in Christ I think
I've glimpsed God's loving heart.
Who understands God's ways
Or where His feet have trod?
Yet I through Christ perceive
He is a Christlike God.

I FEEL HIM DRAWING ME

I asked, "What are you doing, Son?"
He said, "Flying a kite!"
I said, "But I can't see it."
He grinned, "It's out of sight."
I asked, "Are you sure it's there?
I cannot see a thing."
He shouted, "But I feel it!
It's pulling on this string."
I mused, "That's how I'm sure
There's a Father above.
I can't see Him but I feel Him
Drawing me with cords of love."

God showed how much He loved us by sending His only Son into this wicked world to bring to us eternal life through His death. In this act we see what real love is: it is not our love for God, but His love for us when He sent His Son to satisfy God's anger against our sins.
1 John 4:9, 10

For God was in Christ, restoring the world to Himself, no longer counting men's sins against them but blotting them out. This is the wonderful message He has given us to tell others.
2 Corinthians 5:19

Then you will be tortured and killed and hated all over the world because you are Mine, And many of you shall fall back into sin and betray and hate each other. And many false prophets will appear and lead many astray. Sin will be rampant everywhere and will cool the love of many. But those enduring to the end shall be saved.   Matthew 24:9–13

MY CREED

Though ruthless foes play havoc with dreams
And devastation convulses my life,
And though my prospects of peace are crushed
Still will I follow Jesus Christ.
Though fear of war frays nerves to bits
And hope exits to leave us,
And though men's hearts fail them for fear
Still will I follow Christ Jesus.
Though harmonies of nature all cease
And turn to harrowing discord,
And though violence rages in the streets
Still I will follow the Lord.

Yes, we live under constant danger to our lives because we serve the Lord, but this gives us constant opportunities to show forth the power of Jesus Christ within our dying bodies.
                    2 Corinthians 4:11

So be truly glad! There is wonderful joy ahead, even though the going is rough for a while down here.   1 Peter 1:6

Yes, and suffering will come to all who decide to live godly lives to please Christ Jesus, from those who hate Him.   2 Timothy 3:12

A FRIEND POINTING FORWARD

So your back's to the wall
And you can't back up
And you are afraid
You may crack up.
So you tried to escape
But they hemmed you in,
And you've given up nearly—
But you have a Friend.
I've stood where you stand.
I've prayed there and sorrowed
With my back to the wall,
And my Friend pointing forward.

THE CROSS AT THE CROSSROADS

At the crossroads I stood
Pondering which way
For my best advantage
I should travel that day.
Indecision resulted
Until a soft voice
Whispered to me gently,
"Neutrality is choice."
Indecision renounced,
And heedless of cost,
I chose at the crossroads
The Way of the Cross.

And if we think that our present service for Him is hard, just remember that some day we are going to sit with Him and rule with Him. But if we give up when we suffer, and turn against Christ, then He must turn against us.   2 Timothy 2:12

FRESH COURAGE

Distressed with restless pain
I could not lift my head
Until God's voice broke through
And this is what He said:
"Child, if you knew my plan
And my high purpose in it,
You'd fight the fight of faith,
Undoubting you could win it."
A bold resolve gripped me
To fight although discouraged,
And lifting up my head,
God breathed on me fresh courage.

BROKEN LIMBS

Old apple trees with broken limbs
Possess a certain beauty,
For limbs break down from bearing fruit
Beyond the call of duty.
Such beauty of that sort abides
With one of my good neighbors.
Like weighted limbs I watched him break
Burdened with fruitful labors.
If you should pass unmindful why
Fruit trees crash to the ground,
You'll miss the beauty of my friend,
And in trees broken-down.

LOVE HOLDS IT TO MY LIPS

I do not know, I cannot know
Why this deep cup of sorrow
Is pressed so hard against my lips;
Perhaps I'll learn tomorrow.
If not, someday I know I'll know,
For mysteries all explained
Will find me proud, when life looks up,
That I kept faith through pain.
In the meantime, God, grip my hand
And I'll cling with my grip,
Assured I'll sense while drinking this:
Love holds it to my lips.

For to you has been given the privilege not only of trusting Him but also of suffering for Him.   Philippians 1:29

Yet what we suffer now is nothing compared to the glory He will give us later.
                                        Romans 8:18

If you want to keep from becoming faint-hearted and weary, think about His patience as sinful men did such terrible things to Him.
                                        Hebrews 12:3

How to Outwit Adversity

> I have told you all this so that you will have peace of heart and mind. Here on earth you will have many trials and sorrows; but cheer up, for I have overcome the world.
>
> John 16:33

MY CUP OF TEA

I didn't admit defeat
And put up such resistance
That I outwitted it
By denying its existence.
To win was my high aim
Though friends oft thought me beat;
Yet I refused to think
In terms of sad defeat.
Defeatist attitudes
Certainly aren't for me;
Win is my food for thought,
Triumph, my cup of tea.

> *We can rejoice, too, when we run into problems and trials for we know that they are good for us—they help us learn to be patient.*
>
> Romans 5:3

> *Happy are those who strive for peace—they shall be called the sons of God. Happy are those who are persecuted because they are good, for the Kingdom of Heaven is theirs. When you are reviled and persecuted and lied about because you are My followers—wonderful! Be* happy *about it! Be* very glad! *for a tremendous reward* awaits you up *in heaven. And remember, the ancient prophets were persecuted too.*
>
> Matthew 5:9–12

WHY PEOPLE BREAK

An oak tree in our yard,
So stately-like in form,
Stood strong and straight until
It crashed amidst a storm.
Nearby our willow tree
Bowed low to howling wind,
Until the storm passed by,
Then straightened up again.
Like people I have known,
Oaks crash in fiercest wind,
While bowing willows live;
Things break when they won't bend.

AFFIRMATION DURING ADVERSITY

I still believe although I grieve
For loved ones long departed,
Yet I'll not doubt things will work out
If I remain brave-hearted.
I've learned to share each cross I bear
With Christ, my Lord and Saviour,
And that He'll use like some choice tool
Setbacks of life's disfavor.
And I believe I'll soon receive
Comfort and strength in surplus,
And that through Christ all sacrifice
And even tears have purpose.

How to Think of the Christian Life

When someone becomes a Christian he becomes a brand new person inside. He is not the same any more. A new life has begun! 2 Corinthians 5:17

SUPERLATIVES

To walk in love
Is the perfect prayer,
And the greatest sermon
Is to treat men fair.
The Christian witness
Is to help the needy,
And the best example
Is to not be greedy.
The kindest deed
Is to never grumble,
The holiest work
Is to love the humble.
The grandest task
Is a soul to win,
The highest blessing
Is contentment within.

I SOUGHT THE FILLING

Half of my life I gave to Christ
And as you may have guessed,
I felt I'd given more than most,
Yet I found still no rest.
I did not know my Father is
Dissatisfied with half,
Yet in my heart I was so empty
I couldn't even laugh.
When Christ asked 100 percent
I submitted my will,
Having learned the sad truth:
Half-yielded means half-filled.

ALL THIS I GAVE

I gave up a lot to follow Christ,
Like the misery of a misspent life,
And the chains of enslaving vice;
Yes, I've paid quite a price.
I gave up a lot to follow Him,
Like a future bleak and grim,
With self-destructive whims,
And an outlook quite dim.
All this I gave up to have the Lord:
A mind dissatisfied and bored,
With a life of miserable discord
And a hell I was rushing toward.

Don't copy the behavior and customs of this world, but be a new and different person with a fresh newness in all you do and think. Then you will learn from your own experience how His ways will really satisfy you.

Romans 12:2

Once you were less than nothing; now you are God's own. Once you knew very little of God's kindness; now your very lives have been changed by it. 1 Peter 2:10

And what pity He felt for the crowds that came, because their problems were so great and they didn't know what to do or where to go for help. They were like sheep without a shepherd. "The harvest is so great, and the workers are so few," He told His disciples. "So pray to the one in charge of the harvesting, and ask Him to recruit more workers for His harvest fields."

Matthew 9:36–38

LET MY HEART BREAK

I prayed, "Lord, teach me how
To keep my heart from breaking
When I see people starving
In ghettos godforsaken.
And help me not to grieve
When on some far-off ground
Our army scores a victory
And bombs their cities down."
Christ wept, "But you forget
Their pains and grief I bear—
I feel the hurt of millions—
I'm crushed with earth's despair.
My heart is always breaking—
I still must mount my cross
Because so few disciples
Feel heartbreak for the lost."
I cried in shame, "Dear Lord,
No longer in mere token
Will I claim to be a Christian
Until my heart be broken."

FORGIVE MY INDIFFERENCE

I'd see him standing there
Busy pumping gas,
Always carefree and waving
At everyone who passed.
I hardly knew his name
And would never have guessed
He was planning suicide,
But last night he met death.
How strange I never witnessed
Of God's great love for him.
We talked of such small things.
I've mostly forgotten them.
Lord, forgive my indifference,
And when I pass that station
Remind me of others
In need of Thy salvation.

This suffering is all part of the work God has given you. Christ, who suffered for you, is your example. Follow in His steps. 1 Peter 2:21

Look after each other so that not one of you will fail to find God's best blessings. Watch out that no bitterness takes root among you, for as it springs up it causes deep trouble, hurting many in their spiritual lives.

Hebrews 12:15

Out in the woodlands
I'm enraptured to hear
The symphony of birds
In the spring of the year.
But oft I enquire
What a bad mistake
If only the gifted
Did a melody make.
The springtime symphony
Would all be ended
If only the gifted sang
And only if they blended.
God has a symphony
And to heaven it rings
When people sing together
No matter how we sing.
Sweet is the harmony
And things sound better
When all people everywhere
Try to sing together.

How to Think of Nature's God

He created everything there is—nothing exists that He
didn't make. Eternal life is in Him, and this life gives
light to all mankind.   John 1:3, 4

A MIRACLE EVERY MORNING

Today I saw God make the morning
First, he pulled back the drapes
And dawn came chasing darkness
And shadows of many shapes.
Splinters of gold filtered through
The arch of blue-tint sky
And silence with eloquence shouted
Before the sun caught fire.
I wonder why so very seldom
I've seen God push asunder
The curtains of night and await
Sunrise booming like thunder.
I wish the world every day
Could see our God performing,
And witness the miracle divine
Of God making the morning.

GOD REMEMBERS

I placed them here
Crisp bulbs so brown
And shoved them deep
Into the ground.
In haste I failed
To mark the spot,
And as days passed
I soon forgot.
But I, surprised,
When weeks marched by,
Saw tulips growing
Half knee-high.
I guess God marks
Bulbs planned for spring:
It's great how He
Remembers things.

*God's Son shines out with God's glory, and all
that God's Son is and does marks Him as God.
He regulates the universe by the mighty power
of His command. He is the one who died to
cleanse us and clear our record of all sin, and
then sat down in highest honor beside the
great God of heaven.*   Hebrews 1:3

*And if God cares so wonderfully for flowers
that are here today and gone tomorrow, won't
He more surely care for you, O men of little
faith?*   Matthew 6:30

How to Be a Better Parent

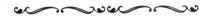

And now a word to you parents. Don't keep on scolding and nagging your children, making them angry and resentful. Rather, bring them up with the loving discipline the Lord Himself approves, with suggestions and godly advice.   Ephesians 6:4

WHEN TRUTH IS PLANTED

I dropped an acorn in the earth
And when the years passed by
That seed produced to my surprise
An oak that brushed the sky.
I planted in my children's hearts,
During tender childhood years,
The Word of God, and watered it
With love and prayer and tears.
Seeds placed in earth produce tall oaks
And that's a law undoubted;
Today my stalwart children prove
God's Word I planted, sprouted.

JUST LIKE DAD

Today he does just as I say
And thinks my words are true,
But soon I know my son will learn
To do just as I do.
Oh, I can fool him now all right
With clever words and sham,
But when he's grown I'm sure he'll see
The man I really am.
Such thoughts, of course, distress my mind
And strong emotion stirs,
Yet it's well known a boy soon acts
Just as his Daddy does.
Let me be pure for soon he'll be
Just like his Daddy is,
God, make me true and kind and good
With motives pure as his.

INDELIBLE RECORD

Each dawn God gives to me
A ledger all unstained,
And then He bids me write
A record clear and plain.
But whether good or bad,
I am aware each day
My deeds recorded there
Will never pass away.
At eve I often pause
Reviewing what I wrote
And sometimes weep because
I cannot change one note.

And let us not get tired of doing what is right, for after a while we will reap a harvest of blessing if we don't get discouraged and give up.
                              Galatians 6:9

Let everyone be sure that he is doing his very best, for then he will have the personal satisfaction of work well done, and won't need to compare himself with someone else.
                              Galatians 6:4

33

So there is now no condemnation awaiting those who belong to Christ Jesus. For the power of the life-giving Spirit—and this power is mine through Christ Jesus—has freed me from the vicious circle of sin and death.

Romans 8: 1, 2

HE LOVED LIFE SO DEARLY

May someone whisper low
When I at rest am laid:
"His life was one long battle
But he fought unafraid."
When I my rest have won
I hope someone will say:
"His life was never easy
But he never ran away."
But if none can sincerely
Declare this by my grave
Then say, "He loved life so dearly
That he died unafraid."

WILL I MAKE IT GOOD?

Today I planned great things
When the day had begun,
But tonight I beg forgiveness
For all I've left undone.
Tomorrow I promise myself
"I'll shoulder my cross—
Make up for neglected duties—
Pay back for the loss."
But will I make it good?
Or live in anguished sorrows
Aware that as today is
So will be my tomorrows.

O death, where then your victory? Where then your sting? For sin—the sting that causes death —will all be gone; and the law, which reveals our sins, will no longer be our judge. How we thank God for all of this! It is He who makes us victorious through Jesus Christ our Lord!

1 Corinthians 15:55–57

Sometimes I want to live and at other times I don't, for I long to go and be with Christ. How much happier for me than being here!

Philippians 1:23

UNAFRAID

I do not want to die
And every passing year
I sense that life is good
And I love living here.
A man was made to live
And we weren't made for dying;
That's why God gave to us
A faith so death defying.
I do not want to die
But one point must be made,
Since I have known the Lord
I haven't been afraid.

And they wept aloud as they embraced him in farewell, Sorrowing most of all because he said that he would never see them again. Then they accompanied him down to the ship. Acts 20:37, 38

MY OAK TREE FRIEND

An oak tree in our yard
Withstood the storms and wind,
Sighing with the blizzards—
Bowing when asked to bend.
Wide limbs for sixty years
Gave shelter from the storm,
Or cast cool shade on travelers
When summer days were warm.
But oak trees have their limits
And living things must die.
One night it crashed and left
A blank place in my sky.
I had an oak-like friend—
A friend of love and mirth,
Whose kindness blessed my life
And then he crashed to earth.
He fell down in a storm
And like the giant oak tree
Where he once stood so tall
A blank is all I see.
How dreary is my life
Since my friend in a tempest
Fell down and left me only
A horizon of emptiness.

You are living a brand new kind of life that is continually learning more and more of what is right, and trying constantly to be more and more like Christ who created this new life within you. Colossians 3:10

IF LOVE SHOULD PASS US BY

The love bestowed on me
By those I love indeed
Is never in proportion
To my deep inner need.
The love that I receive
Is in proportion to
My love for other people
And whether false or true.
If love should pass us by
Let's not blame one another.
We get love as we give it.
I'm loved as I love others.

MY HEART UNBROKEN

Regardless of cost
I sought to avoid
The tragic hurt
Of being annoyed
With a broken heart
From loving someone
To discover too late
My love unreturned.
Alas, I discovered
While living alone
My heart unbroken
Had turned to stone.

How to Be a Better Person

If you love only those who love you, what good is that?
Even scoundrels do that much. If you are friendly only
to your friends, how are you different from anyone else?
Even the heathen do that. But you are to be perfect,
even as your Father in heaven is perfect.

Matthew 5:46–48

THE MAN I OUGHT TO BE

Struggling deep within
Demanding to be free
Is one I hardly know
The man I ought to be.
Too long I've chained him down
With chains of greed and lust!
Too long I've left him bound
With deeds and words unjust.
The man I ought to be,
Too long I've heard you cry;
God, help me free at last
The good man that is I.

FRIENDS KNOW WHAT WE'RE AGAINST

We witness with deeds performed
And with those left undone,
And by the things we laugh at
And what we do for fun.
We witness with spoken words
Whether fair or unjust,
And by reactions we make
To those who don't like us.
We witness—but life is witness,
No matter where we are;
Friends know what we're against
And what we're really for.

A DO-IT-YOURSELF FACE

Like some skilled sculptor's hands
My thoughts fashioned my face
With lines of love and greatness
Or else of sin's disgrace,
Until today I wear
The face I should possess
With lines I drew myself
By every thought expressed.
I cannot blame another
Or God for what appears.
My thoughts and motives formed it
It took me forty years.

*Run from anything that gives you the evil
thoughts that young men often have, but stay
close to anything that makes you want to do
right. Have faith and love, and enjoy the com-
panionship of those who love the Lord and
have pure hearts.* 2 Timothy 2:22

*Oh, what a terrible predicament I'm in! Who
will free me from my slavery to this deadly
lower nature? Thank God! It has been done by
Jesus Christ our Lord. He has set me free.*

Romans 7:25

How to Live With Remorse

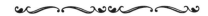

Let there be tears for the wrong things you have done. Let there be sorrow and sincere grief. Let there be sadness instead of laughter, and gloom instead of joy. Then when you feel your worthlessness before the Lord, He will lift you up, encourage and help you.

James 4:9, 10

OPPORTUNITY SCORNED

He turned his face aside
And he was softly crying,
But tears could not be hid
Though he was bravely trying.
I think God planned that day
For our two paths to cross
That I might comfort him
Who wept with such pathos.
But I rushed by that day
Without a second glance;
Yet I've not doubted since
I lost a golden chance.

SELF-INFLICTED WOUND

Did you hear about the man
Who burnt his barns, in fact,
To rid himself of rats?
What a stupid act!
Did you hear about the woman
Who cut her nose off
To spite her very own face?
Sounds like her brain was soft.
And then I had a friend
Who robbed Peter to pay Paul
Because he hated bad debts.
Does that make sense, at all?
I pulled my own roof down
On an enemy's head
To get revenge but it
Left me crippled instead.
One universal truth
I now can humbly boast:
When I hurt other people
I hurt myself most.

About that time Judas, who betrayed Him, when he saw that Jesus had been condemned to die, changed his mind and deeply regretted what he had done, and brought back the money to the chief priests and other Jewish leaders. "I have sinned," he declared, "for I have betrayed an innocent man." "That's your problem," they retorted. Matthew 27:3, 4

A Christian who doesn't amount to much in this world should be glad, for he is great in the Lord's sight. James 1:9

How to Love Children

But when Jesus saw what was happening He was very much displeased with His disciples and said to them, "Let the children come to Me, for the Kingdom of God belongs to such as they. Don't send them away!"

Mark 10:14

NO MORE COMPLAINING

I complained of my children's demands
And of their childish quarreling,
But complaint of petty things ceased
When I lost one of my darlings.
I complained of a six-day job
And of having to rise at five,
But rude complaints ceased one morn when
I awoke too ill to rise.
Ungrateful for the health I'd had,
I lost it and faced death,
But now restored, complaining fled,
And I give thanks each breath.

FORGIVE

When I conduct myself
Like some unholy terror
I've learned with ease to say,
"Lord, please forgive my error."
But loved ones that I hurt
Half-planned or accidentally
Oft wait in vain to hear
Me say, "I'm sorry," gently.
"Lord, I'm ashamed of this:
Please teach me how to live,
And say to friends I hurt,
'I am sorry. Please forgive.' "

WHY THE PRODIGAL LEFT

I know why the prodigal left home.
It wasn't his father or mother,
Or even the hard rules or work.
It was a spiteful brother.
He went to the city to escape
But not his parents or home
It was to escape a brother
Who thought of himself alone.
He didn't plan to hurt his father
Or to disgrace himself;
It was simply the task of facing
One who mocked him when he left.
I think the church has its prodigals
Who leave the Father's house
Because, instead of love they craved,
Church members' envy and grouch.
Let us who love the church
Inquire in all humility
If we've ever caused one prodigal
To leave due to our hostility.

Then He placed a little child among them; and taking the child in His arms He said to them, "Anyone who welcomes a little child like this in My name is welcoming Me, and anyone who welcomes Me is welcoming My Father who sent Me!"   Mark 9:36, 37

I pray that your hearts will be flooded with light so that you can see something of the future He has called you to share. I want you to realize that God has been made rich because we who are Christ's have been given to Him!   Ephesians 1:18

GETTING ONE'S PURPOSE BACK

When life's purpose escaped
And I'd grown too earthbound,
I scaled a mountain path
To watch the sun go down.
I wondered how I'd let
False values crowd my mind
Till I at last realized
My spiritual eyes were blind.
As shadows hid the sun
And night concealed sunset,
I prayed and felt God's presence
As I had never felt.
'Twas then stars on parade
Like sentinels marched in surplus
Across the evening sky
In symmetry and purpose.
Descending darkened paths
By streams that rush like fountains,
I knew I'd captured fresh
Life's purpose climbing mountains.

THE THRILL OF LIVING NOW

What fools we're prone to be
Investing life and strength
In search of future happiness
And going to any length,
To win security's promise
That in some bright tomorrow
A brave new world awaits
Devoid of pain or sorrow.
What fools to forfeit joys
And let sift through our fingers
The thrill of living now
In hopes that out there lingers
A perfect joy tomorrow
As if our God assures
Today can be bartered
For a life that endures.
The present is all we have
And happiness is a flower
That blooms for all each day,
And for some every hour.
Then let me live each day
With joy outwitting sorrow,
In faith that each day enjoyed
Means one more good tomorrow.

But He gives us more and more strength to stand against all such evil longings. As the Scripture says, God gives strength to the humble, but sets Himself against the proud and haughty. So give yourselves humbly to God. Resist the devil and he will flee from you.
James 4:6, 7

And this was His purpose: that when the time is ripe He will gather us all together from wherever we are—in heaven or on earth—to be with Him in Christ, forever. Ephesians 1:10

How to Put Christ in Your Vocation

Make the most of your chances to tell others the Good News. Be wise in all your contacts with them. Let your conversation be gracious as well as sensible, for then you will have the right answer for everyone.

Colossians 4:5, 6

CALLED WITH A COMMON CALLING

Christians have one common calling
To live in such self-giving
That Christ may live and win His world
Through genuine Christlike living.
All missionaries and preachers
And poets and physicians
Confront the selfsame calling
And that's to be a Christian.
All bricklayers and ditchdiggers
And truck drivers who haul,
Are called with the same calling
That missionaries are called.
Even preachers and politicians
Must back up every speech
With a life of Christ likeness
Whether they politic or preach.
Then let all farmers and miners
And athletes playing ball
So live that they may walk worthy
Of our one common call.

MY PLAN

I plan to go to any length
To change some things as God gives strength.
But should I fail I'll then arrange
To just accept what I can't change.
So changing things, accepting some,
I hope to see God's Kingdom come.

TAKE YOURSELF LIGHTLY

You must take your work seriously
But if you should stumble
Don't take yourself seriously
Or act absurdly humble.
Always take yourself lightly
And what friends say of you,
But never take your work lightly
It's serious what you do.
Go through life unseriously
Remembering you'll go berserk,
If you can't take yourself lightly—
But never your work.

Don't work hard only when your master is watching and then shirk when he isn't looking; work hard and with gladness all the time, as though working for Christ, doing the will of God with all your hearts. Ephesians 6:6, 7

If someone mistreats you because you are a Christian, don't curse him; pray that God will bless him. When others are happy, be happy with them. If they are sad, share their sorrow.
Romans 12:14, 15

One Grand Success

Show me a man today
Who, when he comes home at night,
Finds little children waiting
And delirious with delight,
And show me a man today
Who, wearied from business frictions,
Rushes home to his wife,
Thrilled beyond description,
And show me a man today
Who, when he quits his labor,
Thinks only of going home,
And waves at every neighbor,
I say, show me that man
And I'll show you one grand success,
But not in terms of salary—
Just based on happiness.

Well, I'll tell you why. It is because you must do everything for the glory of God, even your eating and drinking. So don't be a stumbling block to anyone, whether they are Jews or Gentiles or Christians. That is the plan I follow, too. I try to please everyone in everything I do, not doing what I like or what is best for me, but what is best for them, so that they may be saved.   1 Corinthians 10:31–33

TO SQUEEZE THY GLORY OUT

In youth and in old age
In pleasure and in strife,
Lord, help me do Thy will
Get glory from my life.
And if I half-forgetful,
Put not Thy kingdom first,
And if for righteousness
I lose my deeper thirst,
Then, Lord, in hot displeasure,
Purge me from fear and doubt,
By crushing me if needed
To squeeze Thy glory out.

For God is at work within you, helping you want to obey Him, and then helping you do what He wants. In everything you do, stay away from complaining and arguing, So that no one can speak a word of blame against you. You are to live clean, innocent lives as children of God in a dark world full of people who are crooked and stubborn. Shine out among them like beacon lights.   Philippians 2:13–15

Indeed, your love is already strong toward all the Christian brothers throughout your whole nation. Even so, dear friends, we beg you to love them more and more.

1 Thessalonians 4:10

RESOLVED

When others scuttle courage
I'll try to keep mine,
And when they dismiss kindness
Lord, please keep me kind.
When friends embrace doubts
I'll increase my faith,
And when all lose their patience
Lord, teach me to wait.
When men delight in evil
I'll cling to upright living,
When no one takes the cross,
Lord Jesus, make me willing.

LIFE WILL TURN OUT RIGHT

Most things turn out for good,
And if you'll wait you'll see
The Lord will work things out.
At least He did for me.
Tough times turn out for good
If you are sure you're His,
And life will seem worthwhile.
At least to me it is.
Bad things turn out for good
Although you cannot see
How God can use all things.
Yet He's done that for me.

For I am not ashamed of this Good News about Christ. It is God's powerful method of bringing all who believe it to heaven. This message was preached first to the Jews alone, but now everyone is invited to come to God in this same way. This Good News tells us that God makes us ready for heaven—makes us right in God's sight—when we put our faith and trust in Christ to save us. This is accomplished from start to finish by faith. As the Scripture says it, "The man who finds life will find it through trusting God."

Romans 1:16, 17

LONELINESS IS ESSENTIAL

I've felt the sting of loneliness
And though it seems quite odd,
Loneliness was essential
For me to find my God.
No doubt I would have continued
To live without God's favor,
Yet I in loneliness was driven
To friendship with my Saviour.
I wonder if any person
Could ever find salvation
If he were never lonely
Or experienced alienation.
In gladness I walk with Jesus
Where once I lonely trod.
In all things God works for good.
Aloneness showed me God.

THE WHISPERINGS OF GOD

I walked apart from Christ
Lest He demand of me
That I in His footsteps
Tread paths I feared to see.
But what a price I paid
To walk from Christ apart—
Sin shriveled up my soul,
Doubt petrified my heart.
"Forgive! Forgive! Forgive!"
I prayed with lifted hands,
"And I'll follow undoubting
Wherever you command."
He answered my prayer that I
May tread as I once trod—
So close that I now hear
The whisperings of my God.

"And you know where I am going and how to get there." "No, we don't," Thomas said. "We haven't any idea where You are going, so how can we know the way?" Jesus told him, "I am the Way—yes, and the Truth and the Life. No one can get to the Father except by means of Me."

John 14:4–6

How to Testify to God's Love

And God has chosen me to be His missionary, to preach to the Gentiles and teach them. That is why I am suffering here in jail and I am certainly not ashamed of it, for I know the one in whom I trust, and I am sure that He is able to safely guard all that I have given Him until the day of His return.   2 Timothy 1:11, 12

THANKS TO THE GRACE OF GOD

I am not all I hope to be;
There're paths I've never trod
But I'm not what I used to be
Due to the Grace of God.
And I'm not what I shall become
Before I'm 'neath the sod,
But I'm not what I used to be,
Thanks to the Grace of God.
I am not what I ought to be
But seeing lost souls plod
I cry aloud, "Lord, there go I
But for the Grace of God."
God knows I'm not what I once was;
"Lord, use Thy chastening rod
'Til I become what you have planned,
Thanks to the Grace of God."

A PERSON-MINDED GOD

God is a person-minded God
And all His thoughts and deeds
Are centered on His people
And on our personal needs.
He knows our deep heart agony
And weeps when I shed tears—
I think He shares my fright
When I'm possessed with fears.
God loves people so dearly
And knows out of the sod
We're weak as the dust, indeed;
He's a person-minded God.
God loves His people enough
To be touched when we are touched
With grief and pain and guilt;
God loves us very much.

Don't ever forget those wonderful days when you first learned about Christ. Remember how you kept right on with the Lord even though it meant terrible suffering. Sometimes you were laughed at and beaten, and sometimes you watched and sympathized with others suffering the same things. You suffered with those thrown into jail, and you were actually joyful when all you owned was taken from you, knowing that better things were awaiting you in heaven, things that would be yours forever.   Hebrews 10:32–34

But all these things that I once thought very worthwhile—now I've thrown them all away so that I can put my trust and hope in Christ alone. Yes, everything else is worthless when compared with the priceless gain of knowing Christ Jesus my Lord. I have put aside all else, counting it worth less than nothing, in order that I can have Christ.   Philippians 3:7, 8

How to Approach the Latter Years

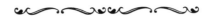

How weary we grow of our present bodies. That is why
we look forward eagerly to the day when we shall have
heavenly bodies which we shall put on like new clothes.

2 Corinthians 5:2

AT EVENING THERE
IS LIGHT

When your steps are slowing
Just keep on going,
Although you have to fight.
When youth departs
Say to your heart,
"At evening there is light."
When strength is leaving
Keep on achieving
Exploits of faith and love.
To those who weaken
Age is a beacon
Pointing to God above.
When night shades fall
Remember your call
Of Christian endeavor,
To follow the Lord
Obeying His word
And you'll keep living forever.

PLOWING STRAIGHT

As a farm boy weary
At the setting of the sun
I occasionally pondered
How well I'd tilled the farm.
I'd ask myself if I
Had plowed the furrow true,
And if the row was straight
As Dad taught me to do.
I left the farm when grown
And now years like a weight
Accentuate one question,
"Have I been plowing straight?"
In life God wants true labor
So when He calls my name
My finished row at sunset
Will find me unashamed.

*We are saved by trusting. And trusting means
looking forward to getting something we don't
yet have—for a man who already has something doesn't need to hope and trust that he
will get it. But if we must keep trusting God
for something that hasn't happened yet, it
teaches us to wait patiently and confidently.*

Romans 8:24, 25

*I have fought long and hard for my Lord, and
through it all I have kept true to Him. And
now the time has come for me to stop fighting
and rest. In heaven a crown is waiting for me
which the Lord, the righteous Judge, will give
me on that great day of His return. And not
just to me, but to all those whose lives show
that they are eagerly looking forward to His
coming back again.* 2 Timothy 4:7, 8

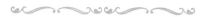
But anyone who won't care for his own relatives when they need help, especially those living in his own family, has no right to say he is a Christian. Such a person is worse than the heathen.   1 Timothy 5:8

GOLDEN ANNIVERSARY PRESENT

With wrinkled, time-worn hands
Half-folded in her lap,
She rocked in her armchair
And caught an evening nap.
And as she nodded there,
My eyes brimmed full of tears,
But they were tears of thanks
For fifty married years.
Her hands were weary hands,
Pain-wracked with swollen joints,
Yet spools of thread lay there
Beside her needlepoint.
"That's so like her," I thought.
These years had not destroyed
Her lifelong scheme to keep
Her hands always employed.
'Twas then with love and tears
I stooped and touched each hand,
And just as she awoke,
I kissed her wedding band.

THIS IS OUR ANNIVERSARY

This anniversary day
My world seems filled with splendor,
For thoughts I think of you
Are very, very tender.
Such gladness of this day
A special gladness borrows
When I think of the life
We'll share through our tomorrows.
For friendship's rich reward
I'm more and more convinced
Will bring to us through life
A richer recompense.
And if the times ahead
Are good as passing days,
Then you and I together
May face them unafraid.
For love we've shared, I know,
If God bestows His mercies
Will ever deeper grow
Through all our anniversaries.

Honor your marriage and its vows, and be pure; for God will surely punish all those who are immoral or commit adultery.

Hebrews 13:4

For a husband is in charge of his wife in the same way Christ is in charge of His body the church. (He gave His very life to take care of it and be its Savior!) So you wives must willingly obey your husbands in everything, just as the church obeys Christ. And you husbands, show the same kind of love to your wives as Christ showed to the church when He died for her.

Ephesians 5:23–25

How to Take Whatever Comes

We are pressed on every side by troubles, but not crushed and broken. We are perplexed because we don't know why things happen as they do, but we don't give up and quit. We are hunted down, but God never abandons us. We get knocked down, but we get up again and keep going. These bodies of ours are constantly facing death just as Jesus did; so it is clear to all that it is only the living Christ within [who keeps us safe].   2 Corinthians 4:8–10

LAUGHTER

I'll try to laugh at things
That daily trouble me,
And grin at little things
Which others may not see.
For laughter is God's cure
For moods of unbelief,
And it leaves faith renewed
And gives the nerves relief.
And he who spreads laughter
To sad men who plod
Is as truly a minister
As the best servant of God.
For laughter is to God
As sweet as prayers we've heard,
And does as much for others
As lips preaching God's word.

So my counsel is: Don't worry about things—food, drink, money, and clothes. For you already have life and a body—and they are far more important than what to eat and wear. Look at the birds! They don't worry about what to eat—they don't need to sow or reap or store up food—for your heavenly Father feeds them. And you are far more valuable to Him than they are.   Matthew 6:25, 26

TO BYPASS DISCOURAGEMENT

Dear Lord, exempt me not
From life and death and judgment.
I can take all of it,
But I can't take discouragement.
I seek not flowered paths
Nor need my skies be fair,
But in the struggle, Lord,
Exempt me from despair.
Grant me such gladness, Lord,
And peace amidst the strife
That I'll bypass discouragement
That saps the strength from life.

SAD HEARTED

It's seldom the work that tires us.
It's our protest against it.
Weariness comes from dreading
And tiredness reflects resentment.
Work alone seldom tires us
For every task that's started
Free of resentments, goes easier.
Dread makes us heavyhearted.

And it is He who will supply all your needs from His riches in glory, because of what Christ Jesus has done for us. Now unto God our Father be glory forever and ever. Amen.   Philippians 4:19, 20

How to Be Very Wealthy

If you love someone you will be loyal to him no matter
what the cost. You will always believe in him, always
expect the best of him, and always stand your ground
in defending him.   1 Corinthians 13:7

BETTER THAN DIAMONDS AND GOLD

To love someone and be loved
Is of all earthly pleasures
The one outshining all others
And life's richest treasure.
To love someone unselfishly
And to be unselfishly loved
Is the object of envy, I think,
Of angels up above.
To love with a love unending
And to be loved the same
Is better than diamonds and gold
And greater than worldwide fame.

WE NEED TRUE FRIENDS

True friends remain true friends
When nothing else remains,
And they remain steadfast
Though circumstances change.
And true friends won't admit
We've done a permanent job
When we have played the fool
Or acted like a slob.
True friends believe in us
No matter what our fate,
And when we fail, a real friend
Still thinks that we are great.
Such faith and love as this
Even to the end
Makes any person great
Who has one faithful friend.

A WORLD OF FRIENDS

The music of laughter
Adds harmony to life,
Transforming to beauty
The discords of strife.
A happy, thankful heart
Adds a tang to living
When you've been forgetting
What God has been giving.
Thoughtful deeds with kindness
Plus a compliment wins
What gold can't acquire—
A world of friends.

*But this precious treasure—this light and power
that now shine within us—is held in a perish-
able container, that is, in our weak bodies.
Everyone can see that the glorious power
within must be from God and is not our own.*
2 Corinthians 4:7

*Yes indeed, it is good when you truly obey our
Lord's command, "You must love and help
your neighbors just as much as you love and
take care of yourself." But you are breaking
this law of our Lord's when you favor the rich
and fawn over them; it is sin.* James 2:8, 9

How to Shoulder the Cross of Christ

Then He said to all, "Anyone who wants to follow Me must put aside his own desires and conveniences and carry his cross with him every day and *keep close to Me!* Whoever loses his life for My sake will save it, but whoever insists on keeping his life will lose it.

Luke 9:23, 24

FROM BEING ASHAMED

The pain of rejection
And the hurt of refusal
Made the cross unbearable
With a shame unusual.
Spitting in His face
Seemed a thousand times worse
Because Judas betrayed
And Simon Peter cursed.
Rejected by His friends
He never felt the pain
Of nails and spears and thorns.
He died from being ashamed.

WHAT OF MY CROSS?

What is a cross? A rack to die on
And a lonely place to die alone.
Why are there crosses? Each one must choose
To take the cross or else refuse.
How does it work? No one can say
But this we know—it is God's way.
Who takes the cross? One's better self
In times when he's fearless of death.
What is a cross? In a world of strife
The cross of Christ is the door to life.
What of my cross? I, too, must choose
To take the cross or my purpose lose.

SOME BLESS THEIR CROSS

Two men on crosses hung
And each man sought release;
One sought release from nails—
The other, inner peace.
One sought escape from shame,
The other turned to Christ;
One asked to be set free,
One begged for Paradise.
One cursed his cross and died—
His life a tragic story;
The other used his cross
To catapult to glory.
Today we each have crosses
That last while life endures;
Some bless their cross, some curse.
What have you done with yours?

So when we preach about Christ dying to save them, the Jews are offended and the Gentiles say it's all nonsense. But God has opened the eyes of those called to salvation, both Jews and Gentiles, to see that Christ is the mighty power of God to save them; Christ Himself is the center of God's wise plan for their salvation.

1 Corinthians 1:23, 24

How to Find Romance at Work

I no longer call you slaves, for a master doesn't confide in his slaves; now you are my friends, proved by the fact that I have told you everything the Father told Me. You didn't choose Me! I chose you! I appointed you to go and produce lovely fruit always, so that no matter what you ask for from the Father, using My name, He will give it to you.　　　　　John 15:15, 16

UNPRAISED WORK

On humdrum days, Lord, make me alert
To do with zest my unpraised work.
Let me perform small tasks unpraised
That go unnoticed for days and days.
Nor let me labor halfhearted like
As if discouraged or else on strike.
Glad hearted let me work with zeal
Until I win one goal for real:
To be like Christ whose unpraised labors
Were done with love for thankless neighbors.

SERF-TASKS TRANSFORMED

The greatness of my Master
Was that while on the earth
He did such common things,
And doing them found mirth.
He laughed with little children
And smiled at friendless faces,
And touched the down-and-outers
In out-of-the-way places.
Among the poor and lonely,
And far from greater things,
He turned serf-tasks into
Work worthy of a king.

For to me, living means opportunities for Christ, and dying—well, that's better yet.

Philippians 1:21

ERA OF GREATNESS

What an era for greatness!
And it's grand to be living
In this exciting age
Of challenging transition.
Great dynasties of history
Recorded on tablets and stones,
Possessed less than half
Of the greatness of our own.
Yet complaining pessimists
Say nothing now is great,
And that for daring exploits
We've all been born too late.
Yet I am convinced
Of all ages sublime
We've been born into
Earth's most exciting time.
What an era for greatness!
And let all future ages
Realize we met the challenge
When they read history's pages.

Remember what Christ taught and. let His words enrich your lives and make you wise; teach them to each other and sing them out in psalms and hymns and spiritual songs, singing to the Lord with thankful hearts. And whatever you do or say, let it be as a representative of the Lord Jesus, and come with Him into the presence of God the Father to give Him your thanks.　　Colossians 3:16, 17

The Glory and the Brevity

A certain glory gleams
And a softness shines
Bathing a tired world
At evening time.
Earth seems resplendent
More than all the rest
When shadows lengthen
And the sun sinks in the west.
I've bathed in the glory
Of the sun's last favor
Warming my tired body
After a long day's labor.
But it's all so brief
Like an evening song,
And the glory scatters
As darkness comes on.
So may the brevity of my life
As the shadows grow long
Be resplendent with beauty
Like an evening song.

How to Solve Agnostic Problems

Don't be misled; remember that you can't ignore God and get away with it: a man will always reap just the kind of crop he sows! If he sows to please his own wrong desires, he will be planting seeds of evil and he will surely reap a harvest of spiritual decay and death; but if he plants the good things of the Spirit, he will reap the everlasting life which the Holy Spirit gives him.

Galatians 6:7, 8

WAR IS INEVITABLE

He said, "If war comes again
I can't believe in God!"
And I said, "War must begin
For me to believe in God."
He laughed, "Illogical reasoning!"
I answered, "History's bloodbaths
Are but the aftermath
Of greed, envy, and treason."
He said, "You take it for granted?"
I said, "The law of sowing and reaping
Applies to peace and war,
And the seeds of war are already planted.
In the thirties an angry Hitler
With words, prejudiced and evil,
Sowed the seeds that inspired
The World War II genocide,
And civilization's upheaval.
For every effect there's a cause,
And for decades nations have sown
Malice and contempt of laws,
And the harvest is not unknown.
As we build deadlier bombs
And fight the cold war of nerves
The law of cause and effect
States we'll get the war we deserve.
Prepare for the holocaust,
I say it as I weep;
War is an inevitable consequence
As we sow we shall reap."

IT'S AT THE CROSS

Does God really care for His earth
Where war and grief outweigh mirth?
Does He think very much of us here
Where crime and pollution spread fear?
Does He know about these awful times
When corruption oozes like slime?
Sometimes when we offer our prayers
I'm prone to ask, "Does He care?"
Except for a cross on a green hill
I'm not quite sure how I'd feel.
Except for a Book that says He grieves
I'm not sure what I'd believe.
Except for His church that really shares
I doubt I'd believe God really cares.
Can one be sure from viewing earth
God cares about His universe?
Only at the cross can I look above
And feel assured that God is love.

Praise the Lord if you are punished for doing right! Of course, you get no credit for being patient if you are beaten for doing wrong; but if you do right and suffer for it, and are patient beneath the blows, God is well pleased.

1 Peter 2:19

How to See the Beauty About Us

And now, brothers, as I close this letter let me say this one more thing: Fix your thoughts on what is true and good and right. Think about things that are pure and lovely, and dwell on the fine, good things in others. Think about all you can praise God for and be glad about. Keep putting into practice all you learned from me and saw me doing, and the God of peace will be with you. Philippians 4:8, 9

COMMON ORDINARY THINGS

From sights and sounds unusual
I find my interest shrinking;
Yet common things grip me
And inspire my thinking.
Like bluebirds and finches
Perched on green boughs turning red,
Or snow-trimmed evergreens
Like saints with low-bowed heads.
Flower blossoms, sunbathing,
And drinking beauty up—
Like thirsty boys and girls—
Gulping from a cup.
Like bees toiling endlessly
To confiscate more nectar
From tassels of corn grown fragrant
Along some farming sector.
My eyes behold such beauty
While most men never see
The glory of common things
That give ecstasy to me.

IN THE MIDST OF A STORM

God hath not promised
Weather always pleasing,
Summer without winter,
Sunshine without freezing.
God hath not promised
Only happy days,
Protection from danger,
Fair skies always.
But He hath promised
His mercy sustaining
When into your life
It's sleeting or raining
And God hath promised
In the midst of a storm
His strength will sustain
And His presence will warm.

For all creation is waiting patiently and hopefully for that future day when God will resurrect His children. For on that day thorns and thistles, sin, death, and decay—the things that overcame the world against its will at God's command—will all disappear, and the world around us will share in the glorious freedom from sin which God's children enjoy.
Romans 8:19–21

So be careful how you act; these are difficult days. Don't be fools; be wise: make the most of every opportunity you have for doing good. Don't act thoughtlessly, but try to find out and do whatever the Lord wants you to.

Ephesians 5:15–17

LUCK IS NO GIFT

Good luck to you who graduate,
But don't depend on luck,
For it takes spunk and brains and grit
Mixed with a lot of work.
Good luck to you who graduate,
But it will flee from you
If all you do is wish and wait
For dreams to all come true.
As only those who send forth ships
Should wait till ships come back,
So only those should wait on luck
Who've done their work in fact.
Good luck to you who graduate
And you can count on luck
If you, with all your hopes and dreams,
Will mingle with it, work.
Hard work and luck are twins it seems
And may this truth we learn:
Luck is no gift as much as it's
A blessing sought and earned.

COMMENCEMENT IS A DOOR

Commencement doesn't mean
As it may sound, the end;
It means the starting place,
The point where we begin.
So let us not forget
When we each graduate—
Commencement is a door,
A welcome open gate.
And let us then commence
To live by truth believed,
And act according to
The knowledge we've received.
For life is like a book—
Commencement is a door
That leads from chapters closed
To many chapters more.
So on this new threshold,
Unfearful of the strife,
May our commencement mean,
"Beginning of real life."

Let us not neglect our church duties and meetings, as some people do, but encourage and warn each other, especially now that the day of His coming back again is drawing near.

Hebrews 10:25

In the same way, urge the young men to behave carefully, taking life seriously.

Titus 2:6

Having such great promises as these, dear friends, let us turn away from everything wrong, whether of body or spirit, and purify ourselves, living in the wholesome fear of God, giving ourselves to Him alone.   2 Corinthians 7:1

How to Really Count for Something

Dear brothers, how can you claim that you belong to
the Lord Jesus Christ, the Lord of glory, if you show
favoritism to rich people and look down on poor people?

James 2:1

WHEN ONE LIFTS UP
HIS BROTHER

Despairing of life itself
He stumbled through the snow
Doubting he'd ever reach
The place he sought to go.
'Twas then within his path,
Half-frozen in the night,
He stumbled on a man
Dying in his plight.
With his last surge of strength
He shouldered that cold form
And found in helping him
His own cold blood grew warm.
As one man saved the other,
So it's with men and nations;
When one lifts up his brother
He finds his own salvation.

SHOW HIM YOUR HANDS

Her work-worn hands were drawn;
Her shattered health gave way;
The doctor shook his head;
The preacher came to pray.
"I've worked so hard," she wept.
"What shall I say to Him?
My hands are empty hands.
What will Christ say of them?"
The preacher knew her faith
And said, "Christ understands!
And when you see His scars
Show Him your work-worn hands."

*If a man comes into your church dressed in
expensive clothes and with valuable gold rings
on his fingers, and at the same moment another man comes in who is poor and dressed
in threadbare clothes, And you make a lot of
fuss over the rich man and give him the best
seat in the house and say to the poor man,
"You can stand over there if you like, or else
sit on the floor"—well, This kind of action
casts a question mark across your faith—are
you really a Christian at all?—and shows that
you are guided by wrong motives.*

James 2:2–4

HE LOVED THE UNCLEAN

Untouchables today
Are waiting to be touched
As much as the lepers
Who needed Jesus so much.
We're sent in Christ's place
To touch the rejected,
And share Christ's friendship
With people long neglected.
Instead of the rich only
Let us befriend the mean,
And touch the vile, remembering
How He loved most the unclean.

How to Sense Your Worth

God paid a ransom to save you from the impossible road to heaven which your fathers tried to take, and the ransom He paid was not mere gold or silver, as you very well know. But He paid for you with the precious life-blood of Christ, the sinless, spotless Lamb of God.
1 Peter 1:18, 19

EVERYBODY WANTS TO BE IMPORTANT

For want of love and deep fulfillment
And the need to be needed,
Some surmount peaks like Everest,
And a handful have succeeded.
For need of being appreciated
And a sense of worthwhileness,
Race drivers at speedways risk death
And adventurers risk violence.
Kings and knaves have this in common—
And rogues with saints bowed kneeling:
Everybody wants to be important.
For me Christ gives that feeling.

DEEDS TO MATCH CREEDS

Dreaming glorious dreams
And quoting lofty creeds
Is admirable if followed
With glorious lofty deeds.
But stargazing followed
With tasks half-done
Is a shame to the dreamer
And a blessing to none.
Air castles and dreaming
I know are essential
But ought not deeds match creeds
And exploits match potential.

THE ONLY FULFILLMENT

The only blessedness
A person deserves
Is someone to cherish
And a place to serve.
The only happiness
One ever discovers
Is seeking each day
The happiness of others.
The only fulfillment
Is Christlike living
And bearing the cross
Of total self-giving.

In a wealthy home there are dishes made of gold and silver as well as some made from wood and clay. The expensive dishes are used for guests, and the cheap ones are used in the kitchen or to put garbage in. If you stay away from sin you will be like one of these dishes made of purest gold—the very best in the house —so that Christ Himself can use you for His highest purposes. 2 Timothy 2:20, 21

How to Make the Home Christian

Now you can have real love for everyone because your souls have been cleansed from selfishness and hatred when you trusted Christ to save you; so see to it that you really do love each other warmly, with all your hearts. For you have a new life. It was not passed on to you from your parents, for the life they gave you will fade away. This new one will last forever, for it comes from Christ, God's ever-living Message to men.

1 Peter 1:22, 23

THE HOME TEST

Our faith is up for grabs
And it could go either way;
It could become extinct
Or experience a better day.
And the testing ground is not
In dogmas teachers teach,
Or doctrines we believe in
Or sermons preachers preach.
If faith is up for grabs
Its test is in the home
Where family life is threatened
That's where it's facing storm.
Unless our homes experience
An awakening of kindness,
Then we'll produce offspring
Possessed with spiritual blindness.
Till homes are Christlike places—
More than mere costly buildings,
Then faith that's spread by kindness
Will never reach our children.

Our earthly fathers trained us for a few brief years, doing the best for us that they knew how, but God's correction is always right and for our best good, that we may share His holiness. Being punished isn't enjoyable while it is happening—it hurts! But afterwards we can see the result, a quiet growth in grace and character. Hebrews 12:10, 11

RAISING GOOD CHILDREN

Parents need wisdom
And a spirit of forbearance
Mingled with kindness
To be good parents.
For parents know clearly
They can wound tender hearts
If they bicker continually
And threaten to pull apart.
Dear God, grant gentleness
And forbearance with wisdom,
That we who are parents
May raise good children.

MARRIAGE TAKES THREE

I thought that marriage took
Just two to make a go,
But I am now convinced
It takes the Lord also.
For marriage seldom thrives
And homes are incomplete
Till God is ushered in
To help avoid defeat.
In homes where God is first
It's obvious to see
Those unions really work,
For marriage still takes three.

Your attitude should be the kind that was shown us by Jesus Christ, Who, though He was God, did not demand and cling to His rights as God, But laid aside His mighty power and glory, taking the disguise of a slave and becoming like men. And He humbled Himself even further, going so far as actually to die a criminal's death on a cross. Philippians 2:5–8

HE LOVED THE WORLD TO DEATH

Jesus wasn't religious
In the usual sort of way
Although He walked with God
And often paused to pray.
He disliked priestly robes
And incense in the temple;
Instead He practiced love
And goodness plain and simple.
Each day to Him was holy
And not just one in seven;
His word for God was Father—
Home was His name for heaven.
The lowly trusted Jesus
And vile men found in Him
A friend unlike most priests,
Or preachers who condemn.
Deep was His love for persons
That all His earthly labors
Were spent in going about
Loving and serving His neighbors.
His was a new religion
For He went far beyond
Mere temple worship and tithing
As practiced by some.
With deeds He praised His Father
As well as with each breath
Until rejected and spit upon,
He loved the world to death.

UNTIL WE SEE HIS CROSS

He was not born in palace halls
But in a crude-built manger.
He did not come in kingly garb
But as a baby stranger.
He did not live in public view
But in a wayside place;
The Lord of Life disguised Himself
To join the human race.
How strange they did not know their King
Until His life was lost;
How strange we, too, know not the Lord
Until we see His cross.

Nor has He offered Himself again and again, as the high priest down here on earth offers animal blood in the Holy of Holies each year. If that had been necessary, then He would have had to die again and again, ever since the world began. But no! He came once for all, at the end of the age, to put away the power of sin forever by dying for us.

Hebrews 9:25, 26

Yet it was because of this that God raised Him up to the heights of heaven and gave Him a name which is above every other name, That at the name of Jesus every knee shall bow in heaven and on earth and under the earth.

Philippians 2:9, 10

Don't criticize and speak evil about each other, dear brothers. If you do, you will be fighting against God's law of loving one another, declaring it is wrong. But your job is not to decide whether this law is right or wrong, but to obey it. *James 4:11*

PEOPLE WHO CAN'T LOVE

In the absence of love
And where one is unloved
An imitation of love
Takes the place of love.
For one can only love
To the degree he is loved,
And some people unloved
Discover they can't love.
But people unloved,
And unable to love,
If loved with true love
Can learn to deeply love.

TAKEN FOR GRANTED

We have to nearly lose
Some treasured friend of earth
Before we understand
That person's actual worth.
So let us while we may
With praise and love sincere
Try proving that we care
And that to us they're dear.
And let's share love today
With friends who'll soon depart;
Too long we've taken them
For granted in our hearts.

OUR MINDS THINK TOGETHER

God has blessed us supremely
Not because we are smart,
But because in ignorance
We've loved with all our hearts.
One thing we've had in common—
A love that naught can sever,
For our hearts have beat in tune
And our minds think together.

We need have no fear of someone who loves us perfectly; His perfect love for us eliminates all dread of what He might do to us. If we are afraid, it is for fear of what He might do to us, and shows that we are not fully convinced that He really loves us. So you see, our love for Him comes as a result of His loving us first. If anyone says "I love God," but keeps on hating his brother, he is a liar; for if he doesn't love his brother who is right there in front of him, how can he love God whom he has never seen? 1 John 4:18–20

So you can find out how much you love God's children—your brothers and sisters in the Lord —by how much you love and obey God. Loving God means doing what He tells us to do, and really, that isn't hard at all.
1 John 5:2, 3

How to Profit From Bad Decisions

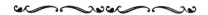

Since Christ suffered and underwent pain, you must have the same attitude He did; you must be ready to suffer, too. For remember, when your body suffers, sin loses its power, And you won't be spending the rest of your life chasing after evil desires, but will be anxious to do the will of God.　　　　　1 Peter 4:1, 2

I DISCOVERED TOO LATE

He seemed rather bored
So I thought to myself
He's rather discourteous
I knew not he was deaf.
I waved and she turned
Unheeding my sign
And I raged not knowing
She was totally blind.
When the anthem was played
I stood but could not see
Why the soldier sat there—
He was an amputee.
Judging other people
And putting them to the test
I discovered too late
Most people do their best.

How is it that when you have something against another Christian, you "go to law" and ask a heathen court to decide the matter instead of taking it to other Christians to decide which of you is right? Don't you know that some day we Christians are going to judge and govern the world? So why can't you decide even these little things among yourselves?
　　　　　1 Corinthians 6:1, 2

LIFE FOR ME GREW SOUR

With vengeance in my heart
For his most spiteful act
I sent him word forthright
That I would get him back.
The grudge I nursed for days
Like most revenge grew sweeter,
Until days changed to years
And life for me grew bitter.
My heart and mind are hobbled
Like crippled feet that trudge,
And life for me grew sour
Poisoned with a grudge.

OPPORTUNITY UNRECOGNIZED

He always expected
When opportunity came
He'd recognize her
And call her by name.
But he waited for years
And never realized
Opportunity knocked daily
But cleverly disguised.
No one ever told him
As he grew bitter and old
That opportunity always
Wears working clothes.

The Real Worship

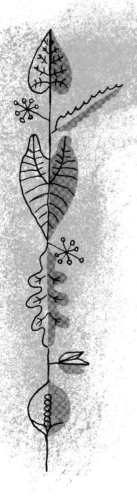

A commonplace task
That to some seems odd,
Is compensating if done
For the glory of God.
A well-dug ditch,
Or a street well swept,
Delights God as much
As a church well kept.
Even changing diapers
Is as sacred a duty
As serving communion
At an altar of beauty.
The best worship is loving,
And serving your neighbor
And meeting people's needs.
Worship really means labor.

For He longs for all to be saved and to understand this truth: *That God is on one side and all the people on the other side, and Christ Jesus, Himself man, is between them to bring them together, By giving His life for all mankind.* This is the message which at the proper time God gave to the world.   1 Timothy 2:4–6

REMEMBERING

Why should I doubt forgiveness
Or that God bids me live,
Remembering when they killed Him
The Master cried, "Forgive!"
Why should I wonder at all
If Christ can conquer evil,
Remembering the victory won
At Calvary's upheaval.
Why should I question at all
His power to love and save,
Remembering His Easter message
Beside an empty grave.

MAKE US GOOD CHRISTIANS

What if to those who hurt you
You show a forgiving spirit,
And yet they continue mocking your name
Determined to smear it.
Good Christians ruled by kindness
Will forgive as God has forgiven,
While most of us find ourselves
By spite and anger driven.
Ought not we learn to forgive
Remembering the price
God paid for our forgiveness
When He won us to Christ.
God, make all us Christians daring
Not only to drink from Thy chalice,
But to forgive repeatedly
Harsh foes intent on malice.

NO CHEAP SALVATION

They drove the nails so deep
He prayed, "Forgive, Forgive!"
Then forgiveness is costly business,
He died that we might live.
They thrust the spear so far
It broke the heart of Christ;
Then salvation isn't cheap,
It cost our Lord His life.
They mocked as He befriended
A thief with His last breath;
Then paradise is costly—
It crushed our God to death.

Who died under God's judgment against our sins, so that He could rescue us from constant falling into sin and make us His very own people, with cleansed hearts and real enthusiasm for doing kind things for others.   Titus 2:14

How to Get Together Again

But now you belong to Christ Jesus, and though you once were far away from God, now you have been brought very near to Him because of what Jesus Christ has done for you with His blood. For Christ Himself is our way of peace. He has made peace between us Jews and you Gentiles by making us all one family, breaking down the wall of contempt that used to separate us.

Ephesians 2:13, 14

DENOMINATIONS DIVIDE

To quote the same creed
And read the same Bible
And pray the same prayers
Christ taught His disciples,
Should unify Christians
And help them find favor
In each other's eyes
Who love the same Saviour.
But our two churches
On opposite sides of the street
Hardly know each other
Or speak when we meet.
I think the name tags worn
By denominations bother
Our getting together
Though we claim the same Father.

Little children, let us stop just saying we love people; let us really love them, and show it by our actions. 1 John 3:18

CRUCIFIXION AT NAZARETH

Joseph, why did you stay
In heartless Nazareth town?
Was there no better place
For you to settle down?
You should have fled that place
Where you were so mistreated!
Surely somewhere there was
A town where you were needed.
Did you stay on because
That's where you'd always been,
And where you owned a shop
And had a loyal friend?
How did you feel when foes
Glimpsed with suspicious eye
The little boy whose birth
Had made the virgin cry?
Were not your hearts both crushed
Ere half your days were done
When neighbors nicknamed Him,
"Illegitimate Son."
Did you not hate those folk
Whose itching ears did hunger
For gossip of His birth
Spread by some scandalmonger?
Joseph, why did you stay?
Ten thousand times they killed
The Christ with slurs and barbs
Before they hanged Him on a hill.

And I want you to know this, dear brothers: Everything that has happened to me here has been a great boost in getting out the Good News concerning Christ. For everyone around here, including all the soldiers over at the barracks, knows that I am in chains simply because I am a Christian. And because of my imprisonment many of the Christians here seem to have lost their fear of chains! Somehow my patience has encouraged them and they have become more and more bold in telling others about Christ.   Philippians 1:12–14

BROKENHEARTED CHRISTIANS

From brokenhearted people
God's brightest glory springs,
And He delights most often
To use poor broken things.
Perfume on Jesus' feet
Spread fragrance afar
When mixed with Mary's tears
And poured from her crushed jar.
And Jesus on a cross,
Broken and dejected,
Blessed and lifted high
A race of sinners wretched.
Nor has one forward stride
Been made since Jesus came,
Except through lives crushed down
And brokenhearted things.
Then let from us exude
A fragrance blessing millions,
Aware that God sometimes
Uses broken Christians.

I am the true Vine, and My Father is the Gardener. He lops off every branch that doesn't produce. And He prunes those branches that bear fruit for even larger crops. He has already tended you by pruning you back for greater strength and usefulness by means of the commands I gave you.   John 15:1–3

THE DIVINE PLOWMAN

When plowmen sink their plows
Into a fertile field,
They feel assured there'll be
A fruitful harvest yield.
God is a plowman, too,
And we each one must trust
He has a hope for harvest
When He plows deep on us.
Then let us let Him plow,
Assured from us He'll reap,
And sure we'll soon see why
He plowed on us so deep.

WHEN FAITH IS REAL

He lost his house with all the furniture
But people heard him sing,
"I have my child, my wife, my life,
And I only lost things."
He lost his business and his wealth
But people heard him say,
"Thank God, I still have all my friends.
Can love be taken away?"
He lost his land, his job, his car,
But still his health remained,
And so he shouted, "Praise the Lord,"
And never once complained.

64

How to Effectively Pray

But when you pray, go away by yourself, all alone, and shut the door behind you and pray to your Father secretly, and your Father, who knows your secrets, will reward you. Don't recite the same prayer over and over as the heathen do, who think prayers are answered only by repeating them again and again. Remember, your Father knows exactly what you need even before you ask Him!

Matthew 6:6–8

WHY NOT TRY PRAYING

When strife corrupts and breeds,
And curses scorch the air,
And you've tried everything,
Why not try prayer?
When gossip blights and damns
And the innocent are paying,
And you've tried stopping it,
Why not try praying?
When vice oozes like slime
And spreads like a cancer
Don't abandon your hope.
Prayer is the answer.

WITNESS FOLLOWS PRAYER

The compassion we feel
And the burden we bear
For the people we love
Is our sincerest prayer.
But if it's for real
And our prayer displays fitness,
Then compassionate praying
Must conclude with our witness.
Pray that self-surrender
Leaves us so emptied
Of self-seeking ambitions
That we'll be exempted
From the shallow compassion
And mechanical loving
That contents itself with prayer
Unfollowed with serving.

I LIFT SINFUL HANDS

I lift my hands in prayer
But not in pride or scorn,
Yet I lift them to Thee
Whose hands were bruised and torn.
My hands have not a scar
Nor have they suffered much,
But I lift sinful hands
That nail-scarred hands may touch.

And in the same way—by our faith—the Holy Spirit helps us with our daily problems and in our praying. For we don't even know what we should pray for, nor how to pray as we should; but the Holy Spirit prays for us with such feeling that it cannot be expressed in words. And the Father who knows all hearts knows, of course, what the Spirit is saying as He pleads for us in harmony with God's own will.

Romans 8:26, 27

Even in His own land and among His own people, the Jews, He was not accepted. Only a few would welcome and receive Him. But to all who received Him, He gave the right to become children of God. All they needed to do was to trust Him to save them. All those who believe this are reborn!—not a physical rebirth resulting from human passion or plan—but from the will of God.

John 1:11–13

THAT LOSERS MAY BE WINNERS

Christ forgot Himself into greatness
And though robed in dark mystery,
He was crucified into fame
And bled His way into history.
Ignoring His life and limbs
He captured the heights of fame,
And nailed to a cross with nails
His name outshines all names.
Dying, He gave us life,
That losers may be winners,
And losing Himself into greatness,
The Sinless saved all sinners.

He never sinned, never told a lie, Never answered back when insulted; when He suffered He did not threaten to get even; He left His case in the hands of God who always judges fairly. He personally carried the load of our sins in His own body when He died on the cross, so that we can be finished with sin and live a good life from now on. For His wounds have healed ours! 1 Peter 2:22–24

We are Christ's ambassadors. God is using us to speak to you: we beg you, as though Christ Himself were here pleading with you, receive the love He offers you—be reconciled to God.
2 Corinthians 5:20

PETER'S SWORD

I wonder why he bought a sword
To slash the soldier's ear?
Could he have thought the Prince of Peace
Could win with sword or spear?
And did he think his deed would aid
The Kingdom to appear?
When will we learn Christ came to rid
The world of swords uncouth?
That He must purge the hearts of men,
Blood red in claw and tooth?
Or else swords drawn defending Christ
Will kill the Prince of Truth?

WE MAY CATCH UP WITH HIM

So skeptics fear this age
Has left the Christ behind,
And that His ancient thoughts
Insult the modern mind.
Well, I have news for them
Which history long has hinted;
Columns of progress march
Behind bruised feet, nail-printed.
We may catch up with Him
Yet skeptics still will hunt
New ways to update Christ,
Not knowing He's out front.

How to Listen to a Sermon

We try to live in such a way that no one will ever be offended or kept back from finding the Lord by the way we act, so that no one can find fault with us and blame it on the Lord. In fact, in everything we do we try to show that we are true ministers of God. We patiently endure suffering and hardship and trouble of every kind.

2 Corinthians 6:3, 4

RECAPTURING THE GLORY

The romance of preaching had fled,
Yet weekly he gave birth
To the very best sermon he could
Although he doubted its worth.
Yet dutifully he preached God's word
And once when his message ended
He soon withdrew to his study
Depressed and unbefriended.
Presently one knocked and entered
With heart, shattered and broken,
And she told of a hope restored
Through words which he had spoken.
That day the preacher recaptured
The lost romance and glory
Of being a spokesman for God,
Retelling the old, old story.

After that, we will be able to preach the Good News to other cities that are far beyond you, where no one else is working; then there will be no question about being in someone else's field. As the Scriptures say, "If anyone is going to boast, let him boast about what the Lord has done and not about himself." When someone boasts about himself and how well he has done, it doesn't count for much. But when the Lord commends him, that's different!

2 Corinthians 10:16–18

A PLACE FOR PREACHING

Groping men, half-blind,
Hoping light would gleam,
Heard one proclaiming truth
And they began to dream.
Adrift, as if at sea,
Men without star or chart
Heard one proclaiming hope
And fearful men took heart.
Men, anxious and afraid,
Whose fears had made them mad,
Heard one proclaiming Christ
And anxious men were glad.

GREAT PREACHING

As students for the ministry
We attended a revival
Where an illiterate preacher
Expounded the Bible.
His sermon and invitation
In a sense displeased us,
For it was mostly repetition,
"Come to Jesus, Come to Jesus!"
Next day we told our professor.
He asked, "Did souls come seeking?"
We said, "Many accepted Christ."
He smiled, "What great preaching!"

How to Live Through the Revolution

Be careful how you behave among your unsaved neighbors; for then, even if they are suspicious of you and talk against you, they will end up praising God for your good works when Christ returns. For the Lord's sake, obey every law of your government: those of the king as head of the state, And those of the king's officers, for he has sent them to punish all who do wrong, and to honor those who do right.   1 Peter 2:12–14

FREEDOM IS OF THE HEART

Though brave men are imprisoned
And chained with lock and key,
Yet if their hearts love freedom,
Then in a sense they're free.
Though cowards and quislings chain
And imprison the brave,
Yet if they love not freedom,
Then in a sense they're slaves.
Freedom is only of the heart.
Then let no one hope to find
It in the Bill of Rights
Unless it's in his mind.

WHERE IS OUR NATION'S PRIDE

I prayed, "Lord make us proud
Of this great land we cherish,
Lest we uncaring let
America perish."
God wept, "I, too, desire
This land in peace to live
In greatness, strength, and pride,
But it's not mine to give."
"Why then our woes?" I begged.
He said, "Lives lived untrue,
Plus greed and sloth have killed
The pride your fathers knew."

MASQUERADE PARTY

Our enemies have devised a plan
To abolish our way of living
Here in America,
And incidentally, they're succeeding.
Brush-fire wars are blazing
Bankrupting our weak treasury,
While strife within divides us,
And our enemies smirk with pleasure.
Anarchy, disguised, is spreading.
We're being destroyed from within,
Because we're duped by our foes
Who masquerade as friends.

Obey the government, for God is the one who has put it there. There is no government anywhere that God has not placed in power. So those who refuse to obey the laws of the land are refusing to obey God, and punishment will follow.   Romans 13:1, 2

Notice how God is both so kind and so severe. He is very hard on those who disobey, but very good to you if you continue to love and trust Him. But if you don't, you too will be cut off.   Romans 11:22

Now your attitudes and thoughts must all be constantly changing for the better. Yes, you must be a new and different person, holy and good. Clothe yourself with this new nature.   Ephesians 4:23, 24

How to Change Your Life Through Faith

> You can never please God without faith, without depending on Him. Anyone who wants to come to God must believe that there is a God and that He rewards those who sincerely look for Him. Hebrews 11:6

A KEEPING FAITH

Real faith is not a thing to guard
Like some pale hothouse plant,
Nor is faith like a tender vine
As scornful critics grant.
True faith is like a tree with roots
Which stands in storms secure,
And like some giant sequoia tree
Which shall through life endure.
I crave no faith which I must guard,
A faith to grasp and hold;
I want a faith that grips my life,
Possessing mind and soul.

Such persons claim they know God, but from seeing the way they act, one knows they don't. They are rotten and disobedient, worthless so far as doing anything good is concerned.
Titus 1:16

Don't let others spoil your faith and joy with their philosophies, their wrong and shallow answers built on men's thoughts and ideas, instead of on what Christ has said. For in Christ there is all of God in a human body; So you have everything when you have Christ, and you are filled with God through your union with Christ. He is the highest ruler, with authority over every other power.
Colossians 2:8–10

WHEN THREATENED FAITH RETURNS

To know the worth of health
Or anything whatever,
One has to nearly lose it
Or lose it altogether.
For instance, freedom's gift,
If I learn its true worth,
And must lose my freedom
And become a slave or serf.
And so it's true of God—
He can be loved most dearly
When threatened faith returns
And we have lost Him nearly.

WE'VE MISSED THE FAITH OF JESUS

We see so much of misery—
Of hunger and despair,
That we unmoved by it
Pass on most unaware.
Well fed we go to bed
Each night to peaceful slumber,
Untouched that multitudes
Sleep not because of hunger.
Religious as we seem,
One fact is clear and sure,
We've missed the faith of Jesus
Who loved and served the poor.

Let not your heart be troubled. You are trusting God, now trust in Me. There are many homes up there where My Father lives, and I am going to prepare them for your coming. When everything is ready, then I will come and get you, so that you can always be with Me where I am. If this weren't so, I would tell you plainly.

John 14:1–3

WE'RE GOD'S MASTERPIECE

What if some artist took
His greatest work of art
And cut it all to shreds
Destroying every part?
What if some sculptor hauled
His masterpiece in stone
Out to some garbage dump
And left it there alone.
How hardly then can God
From His wise presence fling
The masterpiece of man
Or crush a treasured thing.

I'LL BYPASS DEATH

When I die let no one cry.
You know I can't stand crying.
And let none weep because I sleep
Or say I dreaded dying.
Should any grieve because I leave,
Please know I enjoyed living,
And let friends know I gladly go
Forgiven and forgiving.
Then let none groan when I pass on
To be with friends I cherish;
With my last breath I'll bypass death
Nevermore to perish.

THE GLADNESS OF GOING HOME

Have you ever worked
Until strength was gone,
And miracle of miracles,
You worked right on?
I think such strength girds us
Because we have homes.
Have you ever travelled
On a journey too long,
And yet miraculously
You journeyed on?
I think strength comes from
Our travelling toward home.
Have you tired of life's struggle
When all seemed to go wrong,
And yet for no known reason
Your heart flooded with song?
Such is the blessing of Christians
And the gladness of going Home.

For we know that when this tent we live in now is taken down—when we die and leave these bodies—we will have wonderful new bodies in heaven, homes that will be ours forevermore, made for us by God Himself, and not by human hands.   2 Corinthians 5:1

There Is Shining Hope

Why, this old world would fall apart
If there were no gentle praying hearts
To pray for souls bogged down in strife
That they may find abundant life.
Why, this old world would turn to evil
If there were no gracious praying people
Seeking and praying for prodigals lost
And anxious to lead them to the foot of the
    cross.
Why, this old world would turn to dust
If there were no Christians true and just
Praying with all the prayers that rise
That friends will lead true Christian lives.
So long as there are Christians serving
Our Father God and the world He's loving
And caring for blinded people that grope
I say, without a doubt, there is shining hope.

How to Exit Life Gracefully

Because of our preaching we face death, but it has resulted in eternal life for you. We boldly say what we believe [trusting God to care for us], just as the Psalm writer did when he said, "I believe and therefore I speak." We know that the same God who brought the Lord Jesus back from death will also bring us back to life again with Jesus, and present us to Him along with you.   2 Corinthians 4:12–14

HEAVEN FOR THE UNWORTHY

I'd give my all to hear
Christ say when life is done,
"Enter! You've been faithful.
Well done! Well done! Well done."
But if such words I miss
At the end of the way—
And I just may miss them,
I hope I'll hear Him say;
"Your progress has been slow
But you don't belong with sinners,
So I'm assigning you to school.
You'll start in with the beginners."

IT ALL BEGAN WITH CHRIST

All history's hinges turn
On doors of that rude stall;
All streams of justice flow
From Pilate's judgment hall.
All freedom has its roots
Deep in the Holy Land;
All strength to uplift men
Depends on nail-pierced hands.
Life's purpose, worth, and joy
First dawned that Easter morn,
And every cross makes sense
Since Christ was crowned with thorns.

HIS LIFE ANSWERS ALL QUESTIONS

When I depart let no one say
If I loved God or not,
Or if I loved my neighbors well,
Or duty's path forgot.
Such words seem so superfluous.
My life with all its deeds
Needs not a comment, good or bad.
Then please don't mention these.
At death if questions should arise
Don't answer with suggestions
How good or bad I was, but say,
"One's life answers all questions."

For we know that even the things of nature, like animals and plants, suffer in sickness and death as they await this great event. And even we Christians, although we have the Holy Spirit within us as a foretaste of future glory, also groan to be released from pain and suffering. We, too, wait anxiously for that day when God will give us our full rights as His children, including the new bodies He has promised us —bodies that will never be sick again and will never die.   Romans 8:22, 23

But we have never turned our backs on God and sealed our fate. No, our faith in Him assures our souls' salvation.   Hebrews 10:39

How to Have a Positive Attitude

Be beautiful inside, in your hearts, with the lasting
charm of a gentle and quiet spirit which is so precious
to God.   1 Peter 3:4

LIFE IN THE PRESENT TENSE

What makes one follow Christ?
I really don't know.
Sometimes I think it's thirst
At least I thirsted so.
I was estranged from joy
And a stranger to life
And my thirst was unquenched
Until I met the Christ.
Life in the present tense
And life ever after
I thirsted for and found
When I followed the Master.

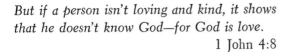

*But if a person isn't loving and kind, it shows
that he doesn't know God—for God is love.*
                                            1 John 4:8

*I have loved you even as the Father has loved
Me. Live within My love. When you obey Me
you are living in My love, just as I obey My
Father and live in His love.*   John 15:9, 10

*Don't criticize, and then you won't be criti-
cized!*   Matthew 7:1

REMEMBERING GOOD DAYS

Tell of the woes you've missed;
Tell not of pains you've borne;
Tell of the good days spent
But not of days forlorn.
For thoughts of happy days
Will prove to be refreshing,
And wise, indeed, is he
Who daily counts his blessings.
Tell not of dismal days
In pessimistic tone;
Great strength rewards those who
Recount good days they've known.

HUSH OUR SOULS WITH LOVE

We'd show more love to others
And never displeasure
If we were not so hurried
Or lived under pressure.
For people are discourteous
When they are worried,
And I'm often impatient
When I'm being hurried.
Lord, lest we hurt friends
In a rushing, feverish nation,
Please hush our souls from rushing
And crown our lives with patience.

It is because I have preached these great truths that I am in trouble here and have been put in jail like a criminal. But the Word of God is not chained, even though I am. I am more than willing to suffer if that will bring salvation and eternal glory in Christ Jesus to those God has chosen. I am comforted by this truth, that when we suffer and die for Christ it only means that we will begin living with Him in heaven.

2 Timothy 2:9–11

THE GLORY OF COMING EARLY

To come late to a just cause
Is certainly to be praised,
But for every question it solves
Another question is raised.
Why do we stand aloof
When justice bows weeping?
And why do we remain silent
When brave men are speaking?
To come late to a just cause
Is to be praised thoroughly,
But latecomers forfeit forever
The glory of coming early.

If anyone is stealing he must stop it and begin using those hands of his for honest work so he can give to others in need. Don't use bad language. Say only what is good and helpful to those you are talking to, and what will give them a blessing. Don't cause the Holy Spirit sorrow by the way you live. Remember, He is the one who marks you to be present on that day when salvation from sin will be complete.
Ephesians 4:28–30

But anyone who is not aware that he is doing wrong will be punished only lightly. Much is required from those to whom much is given, for their responsibility is greater. Luke 12:48

A HEART HALF-YIELDED

Half of my life I gave to Christ,
And as one might have guessed,
I felt I'd given quite enough
And yet I found no rest.
How could I know my Father is
Dissatisfied with half?
I felt I'd given quite enough,
And yet I could not laugh.
A heart half-yielded left me sad
But now life is fulfilling,
For when the other half Christ sought,
I was not unwilling.

HANDS

God takes whatever hands He finds
To do His work today
Sometimes they're strong and youthful.
Oft times they're weak as clay.
God uses hands available.
Sometimes they're soiled and stained,
But if they're willing hands
He'll purge and use again.
Beholding Jesus' agony
I lift frail hands to God
In faith He'll use mine, too,
As He used hands nail-scarred.

You are free from the law, but that doesn't mean you are free to do wrong. Live as those who are free to do only God's will at all times. Show respect for everyone. Love Christians everywhere. Fear God and honor the government. Servants, you must respect your masters and do whatever they tell you—not only if they are kind and reasonable, but even if they are tough and cruel.

1 Peter 2:16–18

AIR CASTLES

He built air castles tall
Unto his heart's content,
For dreams are simple things
That never cost a cent.
On earth he sank deep shafts
And laid foundations down,
And castles that he dreamed
He built upon the ground.
Though dreams aren't costly things
Yet they're of priceless worth;
Air castles must be dreamed
Before one builds on earth.

He died for all so that all who live—having received eternal life from Him—might live no longer for themselves, to please themselves, but to spend their lives pleasing Christ who died and rose again for them. So stop evaluating Christians by what the world thinks about them or by what they seem to be like on the outside. Once I mistakenly thought of Christ that way, merely as a human being like myself. How differently I feel now!

2 Corinthians 5:15, 16

WE FOUND THE RICHER PLEASURE

As brothers we pursued rainbows
When we weren't very old,
For we believed at the foot of them
We'd find a pot of gold.
Of course we never found that,
But found the richer pleasure
Of comradeship with brothers
Worth more than fabled treasure.

A GOOD LOSER

I had to blush with shame
Confronting my accuser
When he walked up and shouted,
"You've been the poorest loser."
Since then I've cherished most
To hear some foe declare,
"Although you lost the game,
You played and lost it fair."
I really love to win
But it's almost as grand
To lose and hear one say,
"You played it like a man."

How to Get the Best and Give the Best

The whole Bible was given to us by inspiration from God and is useful to teach us what is true and to make us realize what is wrong in our lives; it straightens us out and helps us do what is right. It is God's way of making us well prepared at every point, fully equipped to do good to everyone.   2 Timothy 3:16, 17

LIFE PAYS US WHAT WE ASK

When some promotion fails
And strife's harsh winds are brewing,
We seldom blame ourselves,
But friends for our undoing.
Yet blaming other people
For our defeats and errors
Can't hide the fact we make
Our fears, our hates, our terrors.
Each makes his hell or heaven
According to his goal.
Life usually pays us what we've earned
We seldom can blame a soul.

THE BEST GIFT

They baked for their mother
A birthday cake mix;
The girls were nine and ten,
The boy was nearly six.
He couldn't bake cakes
And he couldn't sing,
So when they gave their gift
He had nothing to bring.
But love finds a way
And he kissed her knee.
When they gave her the cake
He said, "Mom, I give you me."

NO RETURN

Retracing old footsteps,
I keep going back
Hoping to discover
My childhood tracks.
But my vision deceives
When blurred with tears,
And memory misleads
When weighted with years.
Perhaps that's how life is,
Perhaps none is to blame,
Perhaps it's God's purpose
That everything should change.
Families circling hearthstones,
Warmed with glowing embers,
Come back from long ago
Only on wings of memory.
I can stand where I once stood
Before I was grown,
I can go back to the house,
But I can't go back home.
For retracing old footsteps
To sweet childhood times
Is an impossibility
Except in the mind.

May God who gives patience, steadiness, and encouragement help you to live in complete harmony with each other—each with the attitude of Christ toward the other.

Romans 15:5

How to Grasp Opportunity

As God's partners we beg you not to toss aside this marvelous message of God's great kindness. For God says, "Your cry came to me at a favorable time, when the doors of welcome were wide open. I helped you on a day when salvation was being offered." Right now God is ready to welcome you. Today He is ready to save you.   2 Corinthians 6:1, 2

OPPORTUNITY UNRECOGNIZED

He waited and waited
But never once grasped
Opportunity was knocking,
Bestowing her task.
Garbed in working clothes,
Her appearance was shocking
To him who expected
Some elegant one knocking.
Yet daily she pled softly
Until he came to the door
And wounded her, laughing
At common clothes she wore.
Then Opportunity broke down
And wept telling why
She'd waited so patiently,
And he began to cry
When he knew who she was
And why he had failed,
And realized with remorse
That ignorance had prevailed.
He begged her to tarry
But she without reason
Left never to return.
Everything has a season!

IF YOU KNOW WHERE YOU'RE GOING

The world will make a place for you
If you know where you're going;
They'll stand aside and help you pass
If you'll just keep on growing.
But they will hold you in contempt
And scorn your lofty morals
If they discover you're content
To rest upon your laurels.
The world takes pride in goals you've won,
And has from your beginning,
But they'll admire you so much more
If you'll go right on winning.
But if you rest content and cease
When others are aspiring,
Friends will begrudge you air to breathe
Nor weep when you are dying.
For we expect exploits from you
And hope you will be giving
The best you have and all you have
In brave adventurous living.
But if you give your second best
You'll reap what you are sowing,
While all stand up and cheer those on
Who know where they are going.

Tell those who are rich not to be proud and not to trust in their money, which will soon be gone, but their pride and trust should be in the living God who always richly gives us all we need for our enjoyment. 1 Timothy 6:17

And having chosen us, He called us to come to Him; and when we came, He declared us "not guilty," filled us with Christ's goodness, gave us right standing with Himself, and promised us His glory. What can we ever say to such wonderful things as these? If God is on our side, who can ever be against us?   Romans 8:30, 31

UNABLE TO COPE

It's not that I thought life was easy
Or I exempt from strife;
It's just that I thought I was stronger—
Able to cope with life.
But I have discovered life demanding
Much more than I'm giving,
And that I'm weaker than I thought
I'm overwhelmed with living.
Intimidated and discouraged,
I'm not able any longer
To cope with life's stringent demands
Unless God makes me stronger.

So my dear brothers, since future victory is sure, be strong and steady, always abounding in the Lord's work, for you know that nothing you do for the Lord is ever wasted as it would be if there were no resurrection.

1 Corinthians 15:58

We know how happy they are now because they stayed true to Him then, even though they suffered greatly for it. Job is an example of a man who continued to trust the Lord in sorrow; from his experiences we can see how the Lord's plan finally ended in good, for He is full of tenderness and mercy.   James 5:11

RUNNING AWAY

How does one just quit?
And what do you do
When you finally give up?
And what do you give up to?
How do you run away
And where do you run?
After trying all these things
I say it can't be done.
A hundred times I've quit
But I still confronted strife,
A thousand times I've run away
But ran right into life.

ONE LASTING MEMORIAL

Within these walls of time
And by God's strength and help,
Each one must carve from life,
A statue of himself.
Soon we'll be through and gone
And friends, bereft, will grieve,
But a statue of our lives
We'll be required to leave.
So let us chisel here,
With every act of duty,
A masterpiece of art,
A shrine to truth and beauty.

And furthermore, we have seen with our own eyes and now tell all the world that God sent His Son to be their Savior. Anyone who believes and says that Jesus is the Son of God has God living in him, and he is living with God. We know how much God loves us because we have felt His love and because we believe Him when He tells us that He loves us dearly. God is love, and anyone who lives in love is living with God and God is living in Him.   1 John 4:14–16

CIRCLE YOUR HOME TOWN

Circling earth for Christ
With zealous mission views
And spanning seas and deserts
To spread the Good News,
Is admirable provided
With every opportunity
We'll span our street to witness
And circle our home community.
Why not witness to neighbors,
And friends dismayed with doubt;
Circling your city for Christ
Is what it's really about.

MY UNREACHED IDEAL

To walk with common people
Is my supreme ambition;
To have the common touch
Is my ideal for living.
To feel and heal men's hurt,
To love their unloved souls,
To lift one fallen person
Is my high shining goal.
To practice what I preach
And feel what all men feel,
Is my supreme ambition
And my unreached ideal.

EACH CHRISTIAN IS PREACHING

The calling of God
To each and every one
Is always the same:
To follow His Son.
And with one calling
Christians tell the story
Each in his own way,
But always for God's glory.
Whether farming or mining
Or cooking or teaching,
We're called to witness.
Every Christian is preaching.

Do you want more and more of God's kindness and peace? Then learn to know Him better and better. For as you know Him better, He will give you, through His great power, everything you need for living a truly good life: He even shares His own glory and His own goodness with us!   2 Peter 1:2, 3

For God has not called us to be dirty-minded and full of lust, but to be holy and clean. If anyone refuses to live by these rules he is not disobeying the rules of men but of God who gives His Holy Spirit to you.

1 Thessalonians 4:7–9

How to Lead a Transformed Life

We don't go around preaching about ourselves, but about Christ Jesus as Lord. All we say of ourselves is that we are your slaves because of what Jesus has done for us. For God, who said, "Let there be light in the darkness," has made us understand that it is the brightness of His glory that is seen in the face of Jesus Christ.

2 Corinthians 4:5, 6

WHY AM I NOT A BETTER PERSON

Of what I am and have become
I'll always have to live with,
For where my body goes, I find
I'm always in the midst.
I'm really trapped with myself
When travelling far or nearer,
And I always just see my face
When I look in a mirror.
Why am I not a better person
So that in my tomorrows
I'll be easier to live with
As I face joys and sorrows?
God, make me worthy of knowing
And daily let me aspire
To be the kind of person
I, myself, can admire.
And help me with my choices
As I face options left
To cautiously choose remembering
I'll have to live with myself.

If I gave everything I have to poor people, and if I were burned alive for preaching the Gospel but didn't love others, it would be of no value whatever. Love is very patient and kind, never jealous or envious, never boastful or proud.

1 Corinthians 13:3, 4

PUT UP OR SHUT UP

When I said, "I feel bad
For the plight of the poor,"
One said, "Your feeling bad
Is admirable, for sure.
But if you feel for them
As you so sadly look,
Perhaps you ought to feel
Inside your pocketbook."
It was then I saw myself
With talk as cheap as trash;
I'd felt bad for the poor
But never felt for cash.

POOR COMPANY

I'd like to take a trip
And see what I can see,
But if I got away
I'd still be stuck with me.
And that's the rub of it
Which haunts me night and day,
I'd still be faced with self
Although I got away.
Why should I fly to Rome
Or sail across the sea?
I'd sooner stay at home
Than have to go with me.